UNDER OUR ROOF

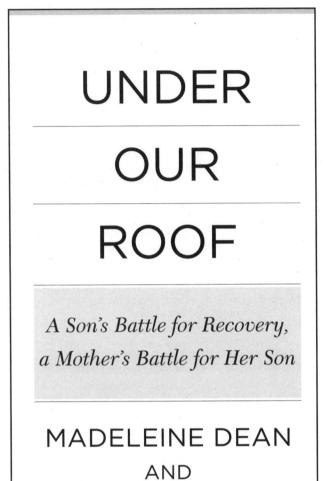

UNDER

OUR

ROOF

A Son's Battle for Recovery,
a Mother's Battle for Her Son

MADELEINE DEAN
AND
HARRY CUNNANE

CONVERGENT

New York

Published in the United States by Convergent Books, an imprint of Random House, a division of Penguin Random House LLC, New York.

CONVERGENT BOOKS is a registered trademark and its C colophon is a trademark of Penguin Random House LLC.

LIBRARY OF CONGRESS CATALOGING-IN-PUBLICATION DATA
Names: Dean, Madeleine, author. | Cunnane, Harry, author.
Title: Under our roof / Madeleine Dean and Harry Cunnane.
Description: First edition. | New York: Convergent, [2021]
Identifiers: LCCN 2020025310 (print) | LCCN 2020025311 (ebook) |
ISBN 9780593138069 (hardcover) | ISBN 9780593138076 (ebook)
Subjects: LCSH: Opioid abuse.
Classification: LCC RC568.O45 D43 2021 (print) | LCC RC568.O45 (ebook) |
DDC 362.29/3—dc23
LC record available at https://lccn.loc.gov/2020025310
LC ebook record available at https://lccn.loc.gov/2020025311

Printed in the United States of America on acid-free paper

convergentbooks.com

2 4 6 8 9 7 5 3 1

First Edition

Book design by Jo Anne Metsch

For Juliet
and
because of PJ

AUTHORS' NOTE

This book is a true story written to the best of our memories. Some names and identifying characteristics of individuals have been changed, and conversations have been re-created as accurately as possible.

CONTENTS

UNDER OUR ROOF

A HOUSE ON FIRE

MAD

When my husband, PJ, is away, I sleep on his side of the bed, nearer the door, as if to stay at-the-ready through the night. One weeknight at about two in the morning, my cellphone rang on PJ's nightstand. I didn't know the number, but it appeared to be local.

For most people, a call in the middle of the night is reason for anxiety. For a worrier like me, those calls are a different kind of jolt—an excuse to race through every worst-case scenario I can muster. I hesitated. Did I want this surely bad news? Still, I reached for the nightstand and picked up the phone.

I worried about all my sons—Pat and Alex included—but Harry, the middle child, was different. Nothing was going well. His hygiene, the state of his room. Most of all, I fretted over the way he'd been changing ever since high school.

Six years earlier, Harry had bounced—I mean literally bounced—into St. Joseph's Preparatory High School in Philadelphia. He was short for his age and young for his grade, yet larger than himself in enthusiasm. At 103 pounds, he went out for the football team as a freshman and made it. Everyone makes it in the first year. But once he got there, Harry became the life and the heart of the team.

Then things began to change. Friends changed, and so did his habits. After four years, the boy who'd bounded through the doors of high school nearly had to be dragged across the graduation line. Harry was pale and sickly—his affect flat and tired, his teeth looking lousy. I challenged him: Why so tired all the time? Why couldn't he get anything done?

We sought counselors and expensive testing, desperate to find out what had happened to our joy-filled kid. And Harry and I fought constantly. I would warn him, irrationally, about what would happen next if he didn't clean up his act.

Tattoos became a thing. He got his first in the months after graduation and hid it under a T-shirt all summer. Something about LIVE TODAY, DIE TOMORROW, with a cross and a crown.

About the tattoo, Harry knew I was not pleased. Yet there was one tattoo—Harry's second—that I could not object to. I remember him coming into the kitchen one evening to confess that he'd gotten it. "Oh, no, Harry," I said. To me, it was just further proof, permanently in ink, of Harry's lost wanderings. But when he removed his shirt, I saw that he had gotten three initials inscribed on his upper back in an ancient, Bible-like font: WRD.

Walter Richard Dean, "Wally," was my uncle and the boys' great-uncle. A Roman Catholic priest for fifty years, he was my dearest friend and lived with PJ, the boys, and me in his final years. So this was one tattoo—the only one—that I did not argue with him about.

Layered over the fatigue and sickness and ink were the stories. One wild story after another, told with a skill that would've made Harry's Irish grandfather proud. The police pulling him over. Excuses for this delay here, this loss there; coming home after a semester at the College of Charleston because the place was too cliquey. And the story, years later, of his daughter's lost baby shower money, $800, evaporated with no explanation. Harry searched his truck and couldn't find the cash. I insisted he look one more time. He went out to look and came back crying. I was crying too.

When I did Harry's wash, inevitably a lighter or condom or something equally troubling would bubble up out of his pockets or call my attention as it banged around the dryer. *It all comes out in the wash*—that's what I would think as I furiously folded his clothes. Before Harry, I had no idea what that expression meant. Leave it to Harry to show me.

I remember going into his room one bright day, a few years earlier, thinking I had the right—the responsibility—to search the room. After all, it was our room, our house, our son.

For some reason, amid the sickening sea of clutter, the thing that drew my attention was Harry's window well. In that sliver of a space between the interior window and the storm window outside, I found a handful of small, stubbed-out cigars. *What a knucklehead!* I thought. *Who the hell smokes cigars in high school? And alone, out the window of his family home?* So foolish, ridiculous, incomprehensible. I was heartbroken. To think of him up there in our house—a kid trying to find himself in the smoke.

I called PJ.

"PJ, you are not going to believe it—Harry is smoking, out of his bedroom! Cigars, of all things! It's the saddest thing."

PJ was silent for a bit. "No, Mad, it's not the saddest thing," he said.

Embarrassment washed over me. I was overreacting again, I knew. But somewhere beneath the reassurance, there was a deeper worry that I couldn't shake. *What else wasn't our son telling us?*

On days like this, it felt like our house was on fire, and I was the only one who knew.

I grabbed the phone from the nightstand. It was Harry, calling on a friend's cellphone. Thank God it was him. He sounded agitated, scared, his voice high-pitched. *What now?*

HARRY

It was a Tuesday night like any other. After finishing a blunt with my buddy Zach, I carefully crushed a Percocet, placing the pill beneath a dollar bill on the flat wooden armrest of the futon where I slept while visiting Zach's house in the city. I smashed the Perc with a credit card, working it carefully into a fine powder before rolling the bill and snorting the line. Then I wiped up the remnants with my finger and put it in my mouth, vigilant not to lose any of the drug— any of the healing.

To complete my ritual, I went downstairs from the third floor of Zach's North Philadelphia row house and lit a Newport 100 on the stoop. I had a dorm room two blocks away at La Salle University, where my mother taught English, and my family lived twenty minutes from the school. But by that point in life, I felt more comfortable off campus and away from family, in a place where I could use drugs as I pleased.

It was a dark, chilly night. As I stood there relaxing and letting the drugs kick in, two men walked up the street wearing dark hooded sweatshirts. They passed the small tree at the end of the walkway and quickly turned toward me. Before I could react, the guy on the right reached for something.

A gun. A nine-millimeter Beretta. He rushed me, and before I could move, he had the barrel in my face.

I don't remember what the two of them said next, but I knew what was happening. I dropped my cigarette and stood there defiantly as they demanded I empty my pockets. When I looked into the bloodshot eyes of the gunman, I could see he was clearly high. Here, I started to really worry. I knew he didn't intend to kill me—or that's what I reasoned, relaxed as I was from the Percocet, the weed, and the Newport. But he could always pull the trigger by accident. He jammed the gun into my kidneys, with his finger tensed just above the trigger.

I focused on that finger. Watching it. Waiting for the gun to go off.

I wasn't emptying my pockets fast enough, so the second man began going through them himself. He took everything: my phone, wallet, and keys. Problem is, I didn't have any money beyond the loosely rolled bill in my pocket. It wasn't enough.

"Open the fucking door," the gunman said, quiet but forcefully. I tried pulling the front door closed, knowing that it would lock automatically. But the guys didn't let me. They forced me into the house, stuck the gun to the back of my head, and told me to take them upstairs without making a sound.

Reluctantly, I did as I was ordered. I took slow, deliberate steps, communicating my surrender. The first flight of stairs brought us into an empty living room with floor-to-ceiling mirrors running along the entire length of the wall. I saw the men's reflection, the gun pressed to my spine, as we made our way around the corner to the next staircase. On the third floor, my friends—a like-minded classmate and a couple of drug dealers from the neighborhood— sat oblivious in Zach's bedroom, probably smoking pot like they'd been doing when I left. Beyond them, there were two other roommates, hardworking college students who didn't use drugs and had no idea what they were getting into when they signed the lease. I wanted to spare all of them what was about to happen, but I couldn't. If I tried warning them, I knew I could be killed.

When we got to the third floor, one of the roommates poked his head out from behind a bedroom door. He spotted me with the gun planted against my head and slammed the door. I heard it lock, then more silence. The gunman led me toward the door of the neighboring bedroom. When we opened it, the room was filled with smoke, just as I had left it.

The hooded guy shoved me into the room and jammed the gun into my temple. "Nobody move!" he yelled.

My friends sat there, shocked. The gunman threw me onto the futon and held me down while the second man stole cellphones and went through everybody's pockets. "Where's the fucking money?" he yelled. No one responded.

Frustrated, he ran down to the second floor to search while we all sat silently. As I lay on the futon, I glanced around the room. My friends looked confused, nervous, scared. Seconds passed like minutes—minutes like hours.

Then a shout came from downstairs. "Let's fucking go!" With that, the gunman shoved me deeper into the futon and ran out. We watched from the window as the men left through the front door and went back down the street from where they came.

My friend Zach, whose house it was, hadn't been home for any of this. He was at the library studying for an exam. I didn't know what to do next. We couldn't call the cops—we had just smoked and the house reeked of weed. Yet after some time and convincing from others in the house, I decided I had to call. But I didn't have to tell them everything.

I went into the laundry room and crushed another Percocet on the washing machine. With that pill, I got the courage to actually dial 9-1-1. I told the dispatcher that I had just been robbed at gunpoint, and she asked for the address. After a few minutes, a police car arrived. The neighbors didn't step outside to see what was happening. I'm not sure they even noticed. Cops were coming and going all the time.

The officers met me at the door and asked me what happened.

"I was just standing outside smoking a cigarette, and two men came up and robbed me, right here outside of this house." It wasn't the whole truth, but it would have to do for now.

The officers put me in the back of their patrol car and drove me around the neighborhood to look for the suspects. They shined bright lights in the faces of neighbors walking the streets. "Not him," I'd say. "Not them." Finally, they brought me back to the house and told me to go inside and lock the door.

The night had been exhausting. An emotional roller coaster of fear and adrenaline. After coming back to the house, I prepared another line to calm my nerves. But the truth was—deep down, in the immediate aftermath of the robbery, I felt good. This moment would define me, give me more street cred, and put me into the spotlight on campus.

That high faded quickly when I realized I had to call my mom. Something inside me said I had to tell her what just happened. I wouldn't have put it this way at the time, but she deserved to know her son had almost been killed, a few miles from her house. The fear returned as I picked up the phone. Somehow, the handset felt heavier than when I'd called 9-1-1.

Still, I dialed my mom's number and waited for her to pick up.

MAD

Maybe I was right to be at-the-ready. Just like that, I was out of bed—scared and angry. In the middle of the night, I drove toward North Philadelphia, toward the university where I taught, and where I insisted Harry attend after he came home from a semester in Charleston. I remember pulling up to the curb on Eighteenth Street and seeing my son alone on the corner.

PJ had been right. The cigars in the window well weren't the saddest thing ever.

Harry slumped into the car, and we drove to campus security. My hackles up—a mother's hackles—I was ready to pounce on any authority figure, however disconnected they'd been from the night's events. Why weren't this campus and the surrounding area safer? Where were the police? A bunch of students robbed at gunpoint, just two blocks from campus? Those were the questions that filled my head. I now recognize that I missed a few. Did you recognize the guys who robbed you? Why were you there in the first place? I didn't bother to ask those questions, because I never got the truth.

I persuaded Harry that we needed to follow up. We called the police and drove down to Philadelphia's 35th Precinct. There Harry and I sat in a cold white hallway, waiting for a detective to meet with us in the middle of the night. The walls narrow, the chairs beat up.

All I could think was that I was lucky: a scared, relieved mother with a scared, reluctant son—but a son who was alive. How many mothers in this city had come here with a different outcome? I wasn't waiting in a hospital or freezing in a morgue. I was with Harry.

Strangely, we formed a little bit of a partnership as we waited in that hallway. Instead of retreating home, we decided to treat this seriously—take the time to report the crime. Maybe the police would find the guys with the gun. Maybe it would stop some of the stickups and violent robberies throughout the city. Save a life.

We spent hours in the station. As night reluctantly turned toward dawn, a seasoned, thoughtful detective took us back to his darkened cubbyhole desk and asked lots of questions. What time? Where? What were you doing? Who were the guys? Any chance you recognized one or the other? What did you lose?

The detective took us seriously. He scribbled notes as we talked. Eventually, he looked up. "Anything else I should know?" he asked.

I wondered the same.

———

PICTURE PERFECT

My friend Lois used to say that a family is
like a mobile—when one member spins out
of orbit, he takes the whole family with him.

MAD

Mine was an idyllic childhood—at least that's how it felt. I grew up in the sixties and seventies, the youngest of seven children. There were Bobby, Harry, Michael, Jimmy, Chris, Maryann, and me. "One for every day's grace," my father always said. I was Sunday.

We grew up during a decade of turmoil. This was the America of John F. Kennedy, Martin Luther King, Jr., Bobby Kennedy; the civil rights movement and the Vietnam War; an America that was frightening, generous, demanding, and heart-crushing. The Dean family felt it all, both nationally and intimately, at home. Every night, our grainy black-and-white Sylvania television played scenes from a nation at war. As a little girl, I learned that we were a nation nightly at war and that extraordinary leaders are assassinated.

Still, our household felt like a suburban version of Camelot: a robust, chaotic Irish Catholic family of nine living outside Philadelphia. At dinner, my dad quizzed us on vocabulary and current events. "Who is Haile Selassie?" (Answer: the emperor of Ethiopia.) "What does 'jejune' mean?" (Answer: naive and dull.) This was long before smartphones or Google, so we seldom got the answers right. I remember my father being incredulous. "If I did not know who Haile Selassie was, I would shoot myself," he said.

My dad, Bob Dean, was small in stature but large in presence, competitive and intimidating with a huge, handsome head to match his brain. He worked as vice president of a large pharmaceutical company in Philadelphia—and influenced the seven of us kids in ways we are still trying to understand. A talented singer, he had a booming voice—embarrassingly so, if you were a little girl sitting next to him in the pew during Sunday mass.

My mother, Mary Eaton Dean, complemented him while remaining quite different: a woman with the most balanced, optimistic, and generous spirit. An only child who went on to have seven children of her own, in part as a gift to my grandmother Madeleine Eaton. She loved my dad and loved her life. She was never bored, and enjoyed showering her kids and grandkids with things she thought they might like.

Throughout his life, my dad's health always gave him problems. He often said that he knew he was in trouble when his weight approached our street address, 208 Roberts Avenue. And his heart was an even bigger concern. When my parents got married in 1945, my father's doctor said he had the heart of an eighty-year-old man. He had Wolff-Parkinson-White syndrome, a condition in which the heart develops a double electrical center, or a "double bundle of His," as he explained. The disorder sets off a very rapid heartbeat in unpredictable moments. There were days when I came home and found my father lying flat on his back in the center hall, trying to coax his galloping heart rhythm back down to a trot. For years, my parents believed he might not live to the age of thirty-five. They threw a big party when he did.

My parents held lots of parties in those years—the era of Dick Van Dyke, Mary Tyler Moore, Archie Bunker. At those gatherings, my father was the spark in a room of talented people, roaming the space with sidesplitting humor and songs. Still, those who knew him would say he was quick tempered and intimidating. On weekends, whether we were at home or visiting the shore, my father made lists of chores for the seven of us to do. My brother Harry always said, "Welcome to Job City." Inevitably, we would finish too few of the chores, and that would send my father into fits of silence and the stomping. We could always count on my mother to add a dash of salt to the wound: "Oh, Bob, you know the boys couldn't paint the railing this weekend, they were busy with . . ."

That was the pattern every time. My father coming in from a hard day of work, hoping for good news at home, my mother offering excuses. What upset me more than being in trouble was seeing my parents disagree. How I wished my mother would side with Daddy instead of protecting us. Just once.

Somehow, I always felt less intimidated by the imposing Bob Dean. I liked being at his side, whether gardening or gathering bricks from houses and hurricanes past on the beach by our family's old house in the shore town of Avalon, New Jersey. My father built those bricks into walkways and driveways that wrapped around our Victorian beach house, complete with a cupola and a widow's walk. I was always amazed, seeing those paths he laid by hand—amazed by all he knew and was curious about, and his detailed approach to everything. In his journal, he logged gas prices and mileages for his cars. He cataloged every antique and tchotchke that he and my mother ever bought or sold. He was always teaching, taking us to museums, historical places, parks.

"Mad, you can be anything you want," he would say. "You are good at math and science. Maybe a doctor. What do you think?" *No way*, I thought. Maybe it was the privilege of being the youngest, or maybe my dad was doing this for my siblings, too—finding ways to give each of us the confidence he thought we needed.

Ours was a fun, crazy house. Seven kids, one dog, many cats, a huge garden, and a revolving cast of neighborhood kids. There was so much going on, and so much going wrong: war, drugs, a houseful of kids to protect and raise. But there was so much going right. Two parents living with urgency, fun, and laughter, generous grandparents an intimate part of our lives, and the company of those they loved.

HARRY

I truly believe that I had the picture-perfect childhood. The middle child among three boys raised by two loving parents. We lived in a beautiful suburban home with a fence, a couple cars, two cats, and a dog. A typical portrait of the American Dream.

My parents are the hardest-working and biggest-hearted people I know. My mom, a lawyer who later worked as a college professor, and my dad, a CEO who followed his passion from a job sweeping bike shop floors to a career building a large bicycle business of his own. They helped anyone who came to them in need—us kids included—and never held back in their fierce love and care. We're a family that hugs when we say hello and says "I love you" when we part. A family who's not afraid to cry in front of one another—my mom generally at appropriate times, my dad at more unusual ones. (Like the moment when Woody and Buzz are reunited with Andy at the end of *Toy Story*.) Funny thing, he tends to remain remarkably composed at funerals.

My mom, Madeleine, stands five foot four, yet in her own way she's intimidatingly strong. Smart and driven. Filled with strong beliefs. Throughout my childhood, she stood at my side, ready to take on the world with me. A powerful love that she often expressed through worry. My dad always felt less intimidating. Despite being driven and always involved in some big job, he was the more laid-back parent, always giving me room to make mistakes. His most common saying has always been "What's mine is yours."

All during my childhood, our house brimmed with visitors and parties and family members who needed a place to live. At one point, my parents took in my cousin for five years; she stayed in the guest bedroom, making it her own, and became the sister my brothers and I never had. And in the final years of his life, my parents built my great-uncle Walter and his dear friend Larry an in-law suite. They lived with us until they died, Wally four years later and Larry closer to ten.

As I grew from a child who once peed his pants in kindergarten to an eighth grader on the verge of high school, my upbringing shielded me from many of the challenges of the real world. My family stayed intact, our finances stable. And though addiction courses through our Irish Catholic family tree, my parents guarded me from it. I felt invincible, even though it seemed there was always a funeral that we had to attend. (Did I mention that we're Irish Catholic?) On a near-monthly basis, a distant cousin, great-aunt, or some other relative would meet their maker, and my mom would load us into the car to go pay our respects. The services usually felt more like a weird family reunion than a somber event.

I had more support and love than I could have asked for as a kid. But as I grew up, a pattern took shape: With all the commotion, all the houseguests and laughter and lives that were busy beyond belief, it became easy to hide in plain sight.

MAD

I was four years old, riding in the backseat of our black 1960 Chevy station wagon, when the report of Kennedy's death came over the radio. I was too young at the time to know what it meant, but I can still recall the sadness—scary to a little girl—that crept over my mother's face as she drove.

For weeks, my parents carried the heartbreak of our nation on their shoulders. They had followed and supported JFK in his run—so proud of this first Irish Catholic president, so drawn in by his beautiful, young family. To this day, I wear a majestic gold eagle-shaped pin on my lapel. My father gave the pin to my mother during the Kennedy campaign.

I took a clear lesson from that time in American history: There was no time to rest. Life was urgent, paradoxically full of pain and possibility. It was edgy, and yet I loved the surprising possibilities in our house. Whether it was my father succeeding at work, becoming vice president while writing and publishing on the side, or the way he and my mother collected friends and traveled the world, I believed anything was possible. My parents seemed so unafraid. They were the kind of people who would go out on a Saturday to shop for a bushel of corn and instead come home with a new car, or a house to fix up.

But this lesson in the urgency of life played out in more harrowing ways. In the sixties, my brothers were subject to the draft, and thus the Vietnam War. Others abused drugs and alcohol. Much of it did not make sense to me as a little girl of six or eight or ten. And yet much of it was unmistakable. I watched as my parents opposed the war, only to see two sons enter and serve in it.

When my eldest brother, Bob, went into the Navy, life at 208 was thrown into turmoil. For an entire month, they lost contact with Bob, and my mother showed up to our crowded dinner table each night wearing sunglasses, as if they could disguise her grief and worry. It turned out that he had gotten sick and needed to be airlifted from the ship. Bob, thirteen years older than I, served as a radioman on Navy destroyers, and then on a hospital ship. Two tours of duty, we would always note. A family distinctly not proud of the war—yet proud of my brothers Bob and Harry. When they came home, the nationwide resentment toward returning Vietnam vets was a stain, a burden we felt on his behalf.

All around us, in our neighborhood of Glenside, the houses were filled with kids and hardworking parents, real-life examples of the notion that "it takes a village" to raise a child. Over the years, I watched as some of my siblings and friends from the neighborhood fell into serious problems. Alcohol and drug use and abuse. Cracking up cars and relationships. Sometimes succeeding, yet sometimes not living up to my father's expectations—and doing so to my mother's heartbreak.

I took all of this to heart. From a very young age, I promised myself that I would not smoke or otherwise experiment with nonsense. I had seen the toll this stuff took on some of my brothers—how my parents were stressed worrying over them. Looking back, it was an extraordinarily difficult time, even in our privileged white suburban world. And so much of it—out of my control.

My father suffered his first heart attack at forty-nine and his second soon after. Each one scarier than the one before. One day around this time, my dad and I were on the third floor of our house, getting a room ready for a cousin from Ireland to visit, when he said, "Mad, I know the statistics. With my heart attacks and angina, people generally live no more than seven years."

I was awfully young at the time, scared and puzzled by his candor.

I had a nickname that reflected something about me: "Logic-aleine." Whether it was the rumors of someone getting in trouble, or the claims my teacher made in class, I wanted to know the evidence before jumping to a conclusion. Even before my father schooled us in logic fallacies, such as *post hoc* thinking, I questioned the connections between this and that. Maybe that's why my father thought he could be honest with me. I guess I have always tried to be logical.

Something else that my father embodied was compassion. My father taught us to be understanding and forgiving. "Remember, paraphrasing a Psalm, 'Men are cracked vessels,'" he would say while worrying about one of us. We are all imperfect.

HARRY

As far back as I can remember, I saw myself as an outsider. I felt uncomfortable in almost every situation. As I watched my friends navigate their childhoods, it seemed that they had it easier—regardless of their circumstances—as though their emotions weren't as strong or unmanageable as mine. Like they'd gotten some inside scoop on living that I missed along the way.

I was born with middle child syndrome, and our family offered the most stereotypical rank-and-file sibling roles. My older brother—"Pat the Perfect," as my nana called him—was a focused, smart, athletic, and well-behaved first child. The only time I can remember him getting into trouble was when he decided to go to the University of Miami over my Mom's strong preference of Georgetown. One day, as my mom and brother battled in the living room, Larry King was interviewing Dr. Phil on the television in the background. As the show moved toward a commercial break, Larry King offered assistance to any viewers who were struggling. "We want to hear from you," he said.

My mom picked up the phone and dialed the number onscreen. Everyone laughed—until someone at the station answered and said she would be on air momentarily. I ran to the kitchen, where Mom kept a small television in a cabinet under the microwave, and found the channel. The call before my mom's was serious, something involving incest or rape. A stark reminder of how ridiculous this argument had been from the start.

"Hello, Philadelphia!" King said after a minute. "You're on the air."

My mom did her best to explain the situation. Her son had been accepted to Georgetown, among other schools, but wanted to go to the University of Miami instead. "He's a great kid," she said, "but I'm worried. . . ."

The host cut her off before she could mention her real concern: that Pat was turning down Georgetown to follow his girlfriend to Miami.

Dr. Phil chimed in. "You said your son is a good boy, it's not like he's going to be running drugs out of Colombia. Pack your bags, you're going to love the stone crabs. You're going to Miami," he proclaimed, infuriating my mom and elating Pat. "He's a quack!" I heard my mom yelling from the other room into the muted phone. My mom worried that Pat was only following his girlfriend. In the end, it all turned out just fine, Pat made it to Miami and went on to marry Stephanie after college.

That's Pat. Then there's my younger brother, Alex. Alex is the "baby" of the family. For as long as I can remember, he's had a special power, the ability to persuade my parents to do just about anything. Whether it was getting them to buy a stick shift car before he could even drive, or convincing my dad that our family needed a boat, if you needed something, Alex could deliver. To this day, he's a creator, constantly coming up with weird, remarkable ideas.

I sat squarely in the middle, about two and a half years separated from Pat and Alex—raised under the same roof, but with a feeling of being miles apart. I was far from being well-behaved, creative, or even contented. As we grew older, I fixated on these differences and sought ways to distance myself from my brothers. Directing all of my energy away from home, toward friends and newfound hobbies.

I vividly recall crying night after night as a kid, never really understanding why. It left me with a sense that I shouldn't or couldn't let anyone know how I really felt. A subtle, growing fear that if people got close enough to see who I really was—the little kid who cried himself to sleep—they might not like me anymore. They would abandon me. I didn't know how this one unhealthy fear could end up directing my life.

I idolized famous people like Evel Knievel and Steve Irwin—men who were fearless and brave, willing to jump the Grand Canyon on a motorcycle or wrestle crocodiles. I did everything to be like them, in the way a young child does. I built ramps in the backyard and spent day after day in the local creek, catching snakes. I became obsessed, borrowing every book from the library that had anything to do with herpetology and imagining life as a globe-traveling scientist. These were my earliest forms of escape. They brought me such relief, a sensation of being freed from myself. In hindsight, they were symptoms of a much larger problem: an inability to cope.

Yet to my parents and everyone around me, it was just a boy's youthful imagination running wild. Something to be celebrated. After all, it was better than being stuck inside playing videogames or glued to the TV.

MAD

When I turned eighteen, my high school girlfriend Joanne Enright called and said her parents would like to stop by our house one evening. They had an idea, she said.

I remember Mr. and Mrs. Enright coming over and sitting in our big living room. Mr. Enright served as Abington Township's commissioner; Mrs. Enright was equally politically active, working for Democratic candidates and elected officials at the local, state, and federal level. My parents were Democrats in spirit, but they registered as Republicans.

As Joanne's parents settled onto the sofas that night, I had no clue what to expect.

Mr. Enright began, "Mad, we have an idea for you. You should run for office. Are you registered to vote?"

I was not registered and did not know how. They said I should register as a Democrat and run for committeeperson in our community. "You'll be running against an incumbent," Mr. Enright said, "but we think it's time for a change in Glenside Ward Thirteen, time for young people to get involved."

I did not know what a committeeperson did—much less what "incumbent" or "ward" meant. "What do I have to do?" I said.

Mr. Enright explained that committeeperson was the most entry-level political position—the worker bees of the party. "If you win, you'll be responsible for working for the party, attending our once-a-month meetings, helping strategize and support candidates. On Election Day, you would work the polls from morning until night."

It sounded like something I might like. So I agreed. I would register and run. As I look back now, I laugh: An eighteen-year-old girl running against a middle-aged man, an incumbent. Who does that?

I asked my dad what he thought. After all, I thought I was pretty busy—a freshman commuting to La Salle University, working part time at Penny's Flowers, a florist in Glenside. How would I ever do it all?

My dad reminded me of a famous sentiment: "If you want to get the job done, give it to a busy person." That would be the slogan of my campaign. I typed it on little homemade pamphlets and handed them out door to door. A few months later, in April of 1978, I voted for myself in the first election where I could legally vote. And I won, with a total of sixty-two votes taking out the incumbent, who had only forty-four. How jejune of me.

I jumped right into the position, attending monthly meetings with the Abington-Rockledge Democratic Committee (ARDC), learning about the dysfunction and divisions within the local party, and the Democrats' strained relationship with the majority party in our town and county.

At the time, our state representative was Joe Hoeffel. At

twenty-six years old, he broke ground by becoming the first Democrat to represent our district since World War I. It was Joe who asked me to take on my next political role, volunteer coordinator for his 1978 reelection campaign to the Pennsylvania House in Glenside Ward 13. Again, I said yes.

For the campaign, Joe had an idea of someone I should work with. A young, newly elected committeeman named PJ Cunnane, who lived up the street. He was tall and slender, with thick glasses and great dark curly hair. A warm personality paired with a confident walk.

At our first meeting, I pulled up to the curb on the 400 block of Roberts Avenue, just a few blocks down from my family's house. Earlier that day, my sister Maryann—always more in the know about people and places—had said, "Mad, you know the Cunnanes, from church. Terry's the basketball star. PJ's the tall one?" But I had no clue who they were.

As I got out of my car, I spotted a tall guy, about my age, crossing the street.

"Hey, would you know where the Cunnanes live?" I asked.

"Yeah, I should," he said. "I'm one of them. PJ. We're right here. Four-seventy-two."

We entered the house together. And from that moment on, we dug into the campaign.

PJ came from a very political Glenside family and had a sense of the ground game that I never did. When we worked at my kitchen table, I would stare blankly at the neighborhood map in front of us while PJ said, "Here's how we will cut the turf, here are the blocks we need to cover, and here is the order we will cover them in." His approach was both confident and optimistic. I could sense he knew what he was talking about. We argued often over issues like universal healthcare—or "socialized medicine," as it was derogatively called. PJ was robustly in favor. I, the daughter of Bob Dean, pharmaceutical executive, was not so sure.

As the weeks went on, my father told me he was skeptical of these planning sessions. "Mad, is this about politics? Or maybe he's interested in Maryann?" He was right to be skeptical, but wrong about the object of PJ's intentions. Sure enough, one night, PJ invited me for dinner. We began dating that fall, 1978, between the work of knocking on doors and trying to get out the vote.

Around election time, a series of crises hit the Dean home. My brother Chris became seriously ill with meningitis while studying in San Francisco, and my mother flew west to take care of him. Then, on November 11, with my mother across the country, everyone but Maryann out of the house, and me out on one of my first dates with PJ, my dad's heart trouble returned.

As I walked in the door at the end of the night, my father called to me. "We'll need to go to the hospital," he said. "You'll drive me, Mad?"

Earlier that evening, he was leaning over to feed one of the cats when his heart slipped into a dangerous rhythm. He could not get it under control. He'd even written a little note before we got home, listing his symptoms. "Just in case," he said. "If anything happened, I wanted to be sure your mother knew. . . ."

We hurried into his Chevy Nova, a good-looking burgundy car with lousy shocks. I raced us to Abington Memorial Hospital with Dad next to me in the front seat and my sister Maryann in the back.

On the route to the hospital there's a huge dip, a valley between two steep hills on Highland Avenue. I was speeding in the no-shocks Nova, and we hit the dip hard. As the car lurched, my father burped, and his heart rhythm corrected. You should have seen him walk into the ER minutes later: triumphant!

All during the drive, he nudged me to turn around and go home. "I'm fine, it's all good, just a scare, just the usual P.A.T.!" Maryann didn't want him to return home, and neither did I. But when we got to the hospital, the doctors seemed to agree. They checked him in and quickly checked him out, clearing him to go home. That haunted me. When we called my mother from the hospital, she urged Daddy to see his cardiologist and asked Maryann and me to keep an even closer eye on him that week. I could tell that the distance was hard for my mother. She always said that she wanted to be at my father's side when he died—a marriage-long promise. It was not common for her to be away from him.

Instead of seeing his cardiologist that week, my father worked hard, as usual. One night, he seemed agitated while paying bills in our too-crowded den. Yet he asked Maryann and me if we needed anything. "Any money for school?" he offered. We did not.

That Thursday, he gave a talk at La Salle about the role of government in regulating the pharmaceutical industry. "Thank you for inviting me to speak with you today," he said, standing before a packed classroom with stadium-style seating. His thirty-minute talk was well reasoned, yet conversational. As he sat down to watch his government counterpart present, I saw my father lean back in the chair and link his hands behind his head. He knew, I knew, that he had won over the room.

On Saturday night, one week after the first hospital visit, Maryann and I threw an impromptu party at our house while my father prepared food for Thanksgiving. My eldest brother, Bob, and sister-in-law Joyce were there too. As we carried on in the living room with a dozen or so friends, my dad finished cooking and went upstairs to bed.

Worried about Daddy, and remembering my mom's instructions, I left the party periodically to check on him. At one point in the night, he called down, and I hurried upstairs to find my father sitting up in a chair in my parents' darkened bedroom. Speaking softly, he explained he was having a heart attack. "Touch my forehead?" he asked. I did, and it confirmed his assessment. It felt clammy, sweaty. He needed to go to the hospital—now.

I called Bob upstairs, and we helped my father down to my brother's car. My dad was never a crier—but he cried lightly that night as he left our house. "Just when I had lost a dozen pounds," he lamented. As we passed through the makeshift group of partygoers, he looked around as if he knew it would be his last time seeing this house he loved.

For the second time that week, we raced to the hospital, this time with Bob at the wheel. On this trip, there would be no bump, no magic burp. My father was admitted to the ER, where the doctors discovered he'd suffered a major heart attack. The lower part of his heart was badly damaged. We called my other three brothers who lived nearby, and gathered everyone we could at the hospital.

My siblings and I sat with my dad in the ER that night, going in and out of his room in shifts. He asked if we were trying to get Mommy home. We were. We had booked her on the only plane back from San Francisco—an unfortunate connecting flight. She would be home by tomorrow afternoon.

Quietly, yet with a strange sense of calm, my father leveled with me. "You know I'm not superstitious," he said. "But bad things sometimes happen in threes." With Chris sick in California, him sick in the hospital, and my mother in the air, who knew what would happen next? "Mad, I know you are strong, and you can handle this," he said. "You will help the others get through—you and Chris." I didn't know what to say.

As time passed painfully, and Saturday night turned to early Sunday morning, my father joked with Maryann. "Allergies bothering you again?" he said sarcastically, as the painful grimace left his face.

Then he told another story. "An older brother asked his younger brother to cat-sit for the weekend," he said. "The older brother cared deeply for his cat and implored the younger to take good care of Sammy.

"When the older brother returned, he asked how the cat did. 'All was well,' the cat-sitting brother said, 'until Sammy found an open upstairs window. Sammy got out onto the roof, but the roof was slippery, and you can imagine . . . Sammy fell, and he did not land on his feet. Sammy's dead.'"

My father continued, suppressing a smile. "'That's terrible, just horrible,' the elder brother said. 'How could you tell me that? And in that way?' Then he asked how their mother was doing.

"The younger brother began, 'Well, all was well until Mom wandered upstairs, there was an open window, and she . . .'" He smiled, waiting for the punchline to land. We, his kids, laughed nervously, wondering why he would tell a joke in this moment. He spent the final minutes of his life trying to soften the blow to come—the extraordinary loss that my mother and all of us were about to suffer.

I remember wanting to tell my father I loved him, but hesitating. We were not a family to say that. This was 1978 suburbia—even between a father and daughter, "I love you" just wasn't something you said.

Nevertheless, with our future so uncertain, I summoned the courage. After he told his joke, I said, "Dad, you know I love you," half asking it as a question. He brushed it off. "Of course, I know that." I don't remember him saying "I love you" back. But I understood, and felt contented: He heard me say I loved him.

After a while, a nurse came in and told us it was time to let him rest. "How are you feeling?" we asked one last time before stepping out of the room. He answered with a smile. "I'm optimistic."

About an hour later, as the four of us siblings stood in the sterile waiting room, we heard a "code blue" from the hospital staff. Immediately, we knew. We raced to the hall outside Dad's room and waited. When the news came, one of my brothers threw a large brass table lamp into the wall. I'll never forget the nurse who came in moments later. "Is everyone okay?" Then, seeing the lamp, she gently said to us, "That's okay, it's understandable. Don't worry, no one got hurt."

Later that day, we met my mother when she landed at Philadelphia International Airport. She knew just by our presence what had happened. I remember feeling sorry that her wish to be with my father as he died had not come true. But my mother did not live in disappointment or regret, and instead found some good in her absence. "Maybe, it was meant to be that I wasn't there," she said. "If I had been there, I would have taken too much of his time. Instead he got more time with all of you."

My father was fifty-eight at the time of his death. I've often thought about how I knew my dad in his fifties but he never knew me in mine. He never even knew me in my twenties. But still I see the extraordinary good fortune in it all. I would not change places with anyone. My father lived his life with generosity, humor, urgency, and love.

As I looked back on my father's diary entries that last week, each day or night he documented the discomfort he was experiencing and attempted a series of self-diagnoses. Perhaps his hiatal hernia was acting up, he wrote, or maybe it was the Butazolidin he took for his gout. This brilliant man was not so brilliant in self-diagnoses—missing what was right before his eyes. In the years that followed, I wondered, was that something we had in common?

HARRY

The first time I saw friends smoking cigarettes—at an eighth grade graduation party—I was shocked. I wanted to be a good person. To offer something to the world, like my parents had always done.

After everything we learned in the D.A.R.E. program, and all our parents taught us, how could my friends be doing this? Hadn't they seen the same photos of rotted-out teeth, and black hardened lungs? Weren't they worried about getting caught?

I always knew the day would come, a moment when I would be confronted with an adult decision like this. I remember looking forward to it. But that night, when the moment actually came, I was caught off guard. Lost between the life of an innocent kid who loved skateboarding and a wannabe grown-up who was anxious to experience new things. Outwardly, I was angry. Visibly so. "What are you guys doing?" I shouted. "You're going to get in so much trouble!" But deep down, there was something else: I was curious.

I hated the smell of cigarettes. They brought vivid memories of driving in Larry's car as a child. Though not blood related, he was my uncle Wally's dearest friend, and their names had become synonymous around our house. "Wally and Larry," the names rarely spoken separately, like Bonnie and Clyde. I can still hear Larry's pockets—always filled with loose coins and lighters—as he ambled down the hall, humming and smiling all the way.

Larry was the slowest, and probably worst, driver I have ever known. Which is ironic, given that he worked as a delivery driver for a local grocery store. The cloth seats in his old Chevy Lumina were permanently polluted with the stench of stale Parliament Lights. He would drive me and my brothers when my parents needed a hand, never exceeding fifteen miles per hour, chain-smoking all the way with the windows barely cracked. I saw how his fingers twitched anytime a lit cigarette wasn't in his mouth. Watching him made it so much easier for me to reassure myself that I would never smoke.

Drinking, though, that was different. A month or two after the smoking incident, I went to a house party where everyone was downing cheap cans of Natural Light. This was different than the night of the graduation party. I'd had time to prepare myself, time to justify my decision. After all, everyone had a drink now and then—even my parents, whom I admired more than anyone in the world. I was excited to try it, and careful to act as if I'd been drinking for years. But the act quickly failed. Two beers were all I could stomach before feeling bloated and completely sick.

Yet again, I didn't understand the appeal. My stomach hurt, and I felt no better than when I'd gotten to the party. But to fit in, I pretended to be a little drunk. For some reason, it seemed important to set the illusion that I knew what I was doing. That I was grown up.

MAD

When I started my own family, I always knew I wanted it to have the life and chaos of the one I grew up in: a robust home filled with unafraid people and ideas. I got what I wished for, and more.

After Pat, Harry, and Alex entered our world, we reached for the unconventional, the uncertain. PJ is the most generous, unafraid man on the planet. Confident, abundantly balanced, yet eager to take risks—smart risks—if they'll benefit other people. He tried new things, applied for jobs that seemed out of reach, and supported my dream to buy and fix up real estate, just like my parents. Yet, unlike me, PJ wanted our house to have a different culture from the one of his childhood home.

PJ never felt comfortable in his parents' home—at least not when his dad was there. To friends and neighbors, his dad, Bill, was known for a friendly hello and the uplifting Irish stories he told anyone who came across him. He would often answer "How are you?" with "If I were any better, I couldn't stand it." But at home, he was not someone PJ could lean on in times of worry or struggle. Rather than comfort or show care when his kids needed it, he tended to lash out. It was his way of coping. He was adamant that his children never mope. Better seen than heard—

and maybe best not to be seen either. He never understood why PJ spent time sitting around, whether he was reading or typing a term paper.

When we got married, PJ silently vowed that our home life would be different. We wanted to work hard and invite others in—and life gave us plenty of opportunities to do so. When the boys were young, my sister and I worried about one of our nieces. Her parents in California were struggling through a divorce. Would she have all she needed? PJ, the boys and I had just moved to a bigger house in Jenkintown. We offered her a place to live, and a monthlong stay turned into five years. It was good for her; she worked, went to college, and later, graduated. And it was good for us.

Then, soon after buying that home, we planned an in-law suite for my uncle Walter, a retired Catholic priest who was growing too old to take care of his house. The youngest of the three Dean brothers, Walter reminded me of my dad in so many ways: smart, funny, wise, and a talented writer and musician. He and my father always argued over who was the better singer, Bob, whose voice rang louder and bolder, or Walter, whose voice was softer and better trained.

Uncle Walter was more than three decades older than I, but in my adult life, he had grown to be my dearest friend. We had traveled together, shared a house in Cape May. I could confide in him the things that were upsetting me, and he would help me through it.

For years, Walter had struggled with health problems, from issues with his prostate to an ongoing battle with depression. And as the boys progressed through school, he faced a cascade of illnesses: Crohn's disease, cluster headaches, a small stroke, and a heart attack that led to quadruple bypass surgery. When I took him to doctors' visits, he always introduced me by saying "This is my niece, my attorney, and my best friend." That declaration got me thrown out of at least one examination room.

At the time, Wally was living in his family two-story house with no bedroom on the first floor. The upkeep was too much. So we invited him to move in with us.

We spent months planning and building. Our former garage transformed into a small apartment with a little built-in altar. Walter moved into it with his close friend Larry, an Oblate brother who never fully signed out of the Order.

It wasn't always easy or pretty. There was gossip and inter-generational fights that none of us were proud of. Sometimes the lack of peace and quiet got to us. But there was love and laughter. There we all were, making it work in our own eight-person group home. I sometimes worried about the effect on our boys—Pat, Harry, and Alex. Would they understand the need we felt to share and help others? Would they resent me for sharing too much? As I reflect on these years, I remember feeling an urgency of purpose. Whether it was taking in our niece, or building the suite for Walter and Larry, I just felt I had to do it, we had to do it.

And so we raced through the boys' childhoods, through elementary school, junior high, and high school. Harry was defiant in his choices from the start. As a three-year-old, he walked out of the local preschool one day, and went up the hill with his cousin Dean. That's when I got a call from the director. "This is nothing to worry about, Mrs. Cunnane, I'm sure, but Dean and Harry are missing." My sister and I raced to the school, but the boys were nowhere to be found. When my sister went home, she discovered them hiding and playing on her third floor.

When I saw Harry, I asked him what was going on. Didn't he like school?

"No, I'm dropping out," he said.

An auspicious start. Harry was a preschool dropout.

Fortunately, elementary school went better. All our boys entered into a local Catholic school at once: Pat, precariously in second grade; Harry, too confident in kindergarten; and Alex,

not fully potty trained, in the preschool. (Sorry, Alex.) Harry enjoyed the school, but as the years went on, its rules and culture
became a source of conflict.

Harry, always the rebel, liked to keep his hair long. And PJ
and I liked it too. His deep brown wavy hair matched his personality and seemed to offer him confidence as he cruised
through later elementary school. Harry was a popular boy—
a kids' kid—but his charm worked less with the administration,
especially when it came to his hair. According to the school's
dress code, a student's hair could not touch his collar; and Harry's hair touched his collar. Not willing to cut it shorter, we
scheduled a meeting with the school's tough, smart principal,
Sister Maureen, when Harry was in sixth grade.

As I walked into the school that day, I was ready to fight for
Harry. I have trouble with "rules" such as this, rules that feel like
rules for rules' sake. And Harry had a history—a problem back
in third grade—one that took months to figure out. He was unhappy in school, not doing his homework, hating the place. We
met with his teachers and had Harry's learning tested. It turned
out he was an auditory learner, using a tapping pattern to mem-
orize and return information. But they had no idea why Harry
was so miserable, falling behind. And Harry wouldn't tell.

A random conversation with a friend—the mother of a girl in
Harry's class—unlocked the mystery. As we crossed paths in a
Barnes and Noble parking lot, she asked, "How are you, Mad?"

"Not good," I blurted out. "Harry is doing lousy at school,
and we can't figure out why."

"It's no wonder," she said, "with those kids picking on him . . ."
What?

"Joanna tells me some boys are bullying him, teasing him for
being liked by the girls."

That was it. I sailed into school directly from that parking lot.
How could you all know nothing? The school prided itself on

knowing every kid, but they didn't know mine. I was mad. Mad about Harry. How could they miss it?

Three years later, as Harry and I waited to be called into Sister Maureen's tiny office, I thought back to that incident. And I looked at Harry now, a little nervous, but with a daring sparkle in his eyes.

Sister called us in to sit around a circular table with child-sized plastic chairs. She repeated the school's hair and collar rule, and I told her I disagreed with it. We would not be getting a cut. She relented. This was one rule where we agreed to disagree.

By the time Harry entered high school, however, a different disagreement opened up between him and me. Pat had chosen La Salle College High School, a local Catholic school, and enjoyed it greatly. When it came time for Harry and Alex to enroll, I figured they would do the same. Right?

Wrong. Not Harry. Harry insisted that he attend St. Joseph's Preparatory High School in Philadelphia. Absurd to me. The Prep was a great school—more diverse and located in the city—but I wanted Harry to stay closer to home.

We battled for weeks.

"La Salle is so boring," he said.

"But Pat's there!" I pleaded.

"Exactly! Pat's there. I want the Prep; I loved my summer camp there. And I told the kids and the camp counselors, I'm coming to the Prep."

PJ had no problem with Harry going to the Prep. This was so often our dilemma: me believing strongly one way—the way opposite to one of our boys—and PJ being open to the thing they wanted. Our kids never knew the toll some of our brothers' problems took on our family—or how that affected us. We had seen families struggle, hurt, and heave. I was determined ours wouldn't end up with the same fate.

In the end, it was my mother-in-law, Joan Cunnane, who convinced me to give in. She argued that Harry should have his choice. After all, Harry was always following Pat—his tall, talented older brother. A hard act to follow—and Harry is not a follower. He needed to be allowed his own path. And so it was: Harry bounded into St. Joe's, taking the school by storm, playing football at five foot nothing and a touch more than a hundred pounds. He wrestled and was among the first to take Mandarin. Always surrounded by gangs of friends.

And then, one ordinary Friday night, sitting with two other couples—our neighbors and some of our closest friends—the other parents got simultaneous calls. The kids were in trouble.

HARRY

High school brought a freedom that I'd never experienced. Each morning, I would take the bus straight up Broad Street and watch how the landscape changed dramatically when we passed over Cheltenham Avenue—the line between our county and the City of Philadelphia. The moment you crossed over, the green trees and manicured lawns disappeared, giving way to smaller homes, increasingly crowded together. Fewer trees, but a lot more action. People moving about with a sense of urgency. A different life, with new opportunities.

At the start of freshman year, I was fourteen years old but looked closer to nine or ten—short for my age and lacking facial hair or any other visible sign of puberty. People always pointed out my long eyelashes and innocent eyes. I had long hair and a terrible sense of style, but I didn't care. I was starting fresh. I had chosen to go to St. Joseph's Prep in North Philadelphia, the rival to the school where my older brother Pat was enrolled. From a young age, I learned that if I did things my way, I couldn't be compared to him.

I hadn't been the perfect student. In grade school, I battled with the principal over my haircut, snuck food into assemblies, and once dialed 9-1-1 from a payphone in the cafeteria, confident the call wouldn't go through without the required thirty-five cents. In the end, it caused quite a scene. I hadn't heard the dial tone, and I hung up in panic after a dispatcher's voice came on the line. I was barely a few feet away when the old rotary dial payphone rang again. I heard my teacher trying to explain that it must have been a mistake, there was no emergency. "Not to worry, we will make sure it doesn't happen again," she said before ending the call. I spent the rest of the afternoon sitting outside the principal's office, trying to withhold a confession.

In class, I did well when I applied myself, but I rarely did so. I despised homework and figured I could get by with doing the bare minimum. I lied frequently, telling the teacher I'd forgotten my assignment at home when really I'd chosen to skateboard instead. I would rifle through my backpack, pretending to look for the printout. I didn't realize it then, but I was practicing for much bigger lies to come.

St. Joseph's Prep felt like an oasis: an expensive all-boys academy surrounded by the harsh reality of North Philly. The bus ride took forty minutes each way, and those forty minutes would slowly change me. I met new friends who introduced me to new experiences. They showed me how to buy alcohol and cigarettes at a small deli off Broad Street, where the woman behind the bulletproof glass never asked for ID. I learned the difference between beer and liquor and everything in between. On the bus, I was free, not needing to censor my wants or desires from anyone. I could transform from a child into a man.

One day, my friends and I made plans for a night of drinking at a local golf course. We went through all of the details: which girls to invite, whose older brother would buy us alcohol. (Not mine, of course. He wouldn't do it, and I would've been terrified to ask.) We schemed over what we would tell our parents to avoid suspicion.

Charlotte, my next door neighbor, agreed to come. We had known each other since kindergarten, and her parents were my parents' closest friends. Having been so close for so long, we shared an inherent trust. Just telling our parents that we were together was enough to ease their minds. They had no reason not to believe us; until now, we hadn't had anything to hide.

On the night of the party, fifteen of us set up near some trees on the edge of the darkened golf course. We had a case of forty-ounce Hurricanes. The malt liquor tasted awful, but it got you drunk faster than beer. I almost gave up—couldn't get over the taste—but when I got past the top cone of the bottle, I thought less about the taste and more about how I felt. In that moment, all my fears of feeling different from my friends quickly vanished. We were one, joking and laughing and checking to make sure the coast was clear. I was drunk for the first time and loving it. And to top it off, we got away with it all. Nobody's parents found out. The cops were nowhere to be found. It was perfect.

On the following Monday, the bus ride felt different. I talked endlessly about how much fun we'd had, and I pushed my friends to decide when we could do it again. My fantasies about life as a daredevil or a crocodile wrestler disappeared. I didn't need them anymore. The memory of that party consumed my thoughts from that night forward. I knew I had to get drunk again. And I did. The golf course became our weekend ritual. For weeks, we did the same thing over and over again—drinking, hiding, laughing. It never got old.

But one cold night later that fall, things didn't go as planned. In the middle of our gathering, the cops showed up at the golf course. Everyone scattered, sprinting away in different directions. I followed a group of my friends behind a building, but when I got there and looked beyond it, I saw a squad car lurking, its spotlight shining clearly against the friends who had gone before me. They were caught. I was drunk, but conscious enough to avoid stumbling face-first into a guaranteed arrest.

I felt terrified. At fourteen years old, having never been in real trouble, I equated an underage drinking citation with the end of the world. Or at least the end of my world. The golf course was flanked by a large shopping center, where I could see the flashing lights of parked police cars, and a quiet residential street. So I drunkenly stampeded through the bushes of a house neighboring the golf course and made it out onto the street. From there, my run slowed to a walk. To get home, I would need to walk past the cops and the friends who had already been detained. I had to act natural.

As I approached, the cop stopped me and asked what I was doing. "I'm just walking home," I told him. Maybe it was because I looked so much younger than my peers, or maybe it was because my friends told him they'd never seen me before. Either way, the officer allowed me to keep walking while he continued collecting information from my friends.

I got away.

My heart was racing. I felt great, even emboldened, until I remembered that my friends hadn't been so lucky. My cover would be blown.

On the way home, I got a call from Mom and Dad. "Where are you?" they asked in a tone that was serious, but not angry. They had been with the parents of two of my friends when they called from the police station, asking to be picked up with their newly awarded underage drinking citations.

"I'm fine," I replied. "I'm at the Acme in Jenkintown." It took a lot of focus to make sure my words didn't slur.

Who did I think I was fooling? Immediately, my parents realized I had been drinking, too. Lucky as I was to avoid a citation, I knew I wouldn't get off as easy at home.

MAD

Harry's friends were hauled off by the police and put through the protocol for underage drinking. Even those with no history of acting up had been caught drinking in that field. But not Harry. Harry somehow escaped, taking off and eventually running into the local Acme, where he lost himself in the crowd of late-night shoppers. As our friends drove to the police station, PJ left to get Harry at the grocery store. He reminded us that he had always taught his boys to run.

I must admit, uptight as I am, I was not so shocked by what happened that night. I knew we would have to deal with kids and the misadventures that come with adolescence. Still, I was sorry for the other kids and their parents and the costly consequences they suffered.

That night, I met PJ and Harry in the driveway upon their return. When Harry got out of the car and started to talk, his voice matched his smile: silly.

"So, Mom, here's what really happened . . ."

"Harry, we can talk in the morning. I'm worried about the others."

"But Mom, really, I didn't have as much," he slurred. "I just walked away." He sounded ridiculous. Harry looked underage for high school, let alone for underage drinking.

"Harry, I think you ought to say no more," I said. "Go to bed. We can talk in the morning."

I have to admit, I was proud of myself in that moment—not taking the drunken bait. I thought it was mature of me to say we would talk in the morning, to wait to decide on a punishment after PJ and I got a good night's sleep. But what haunts me to this day is that I don't believe I ever saw Harry drunk again. That would become part of the puzzle.

THREE

KEEPING SECRETS

HARRY

The first time I smoked pot, I remember feeling euphoric. It gave me all the feelings I wanted without the stomach pain that drinking always caused. It felt almost medicinal. With each exhale that night, I let go of my worries, my inadequacies, my fears.

I had planned that first high for weeks. On a cold night, near the golf course where I first got drunk, I left the main drinking party with a handful of buddies. We knew we had to be cautious, not only to evade the cops, but to hide our new indulgence from our friends. Most of my peers were uncomfortable with the idea of drugs. But I didn't care. My mind was made up.

We hurried into a wooded area near the golf course, stood in a circle, and lit up. After a few minutes and some minor paranoia provoked by passing cars, we came out of the woods and lit cigarettes to cover the smell before walking back to the party.

And just like that, I made a daily ritual out of another thing I'd sworn I'd never do. That's the dangerous part of nevers. The moment you try one and get away with it, you gain a false sense of confidence, a reassurance that your vice isn't as bad as you originally thought.

From there, my high school years—those precious, formative years—became a blur. I was a hopeless romantic, always searching for that next fix. Drugs became like a mistress I knew I had to hide but would risk anything for. I remember thinking how wrong I had been when I declared I would never smoke. So foolish. I could no longer imagine myself without that feeling.

MAD

Something began to change after that night on the golf course. Most noticeable to us was Harry's gradual change of friends. His friend from childhood, Ben, had gone to the Prep around the same time as Harry. He was excelling in school and sports, in everything. But somehow, we were not seeing Ben anymore. Instead of coming into our house, Harry's new friends just lurked at the edge of our driveway waiting for Harry to come out. I didn't know them, but I knew I did not like them.

More than once, I followed Harry to the edge of our driveway to butt in and see what was happening. "Hello, Mark, how are you?" I said.

"Hello, Mrs. Cunnane," he said, looking down. Harry bristled.

"And who is this, Harry?"

"Uh, that's Mark's girlfriend, Michelle."

"Hello, Michelle, how are you?"

None of them would look directly at me. They just meandered into the street and climbed into a car that looked as beat up as they did. But my message had been sent: *Whatever the hell you are all up to, it stinks. And you are not fooling me.* I remember thinking—and probably asking Harry, too—"Where's Ben? What happened to Ben?"

Around that time, I had this image of Harry and his classmates on separate conveyor belts of life. Some, like Ben and others, moved speedily forward. Others, like Harry, had slipped slowly and maddeningly behind.

Each year, PJ and I attended "back to school" nights, at which parents would walk the halls and meet with our children's teachers. In meeting after meeting, we learned of Harry's slide. His grades slipping, his passion for sports gone. Trying to figure out the reasons for the reversals. What had happened to the kid who left grade school ready to take the world by storm?

HARRY

It starts with something small. A white lie or a minor self-deception. But things snowball from there.

At first, the drugs made me happier than I had ever been. I wasn't using against my will. It was the opposite. I felt in control, like I was living life exactly how I wanted, abandoning the sheltered childhood that my parents had worked so hard to construct. But this was my life. I saw no need to consider anyone else's perspective or heed anybody's advice.

That's not to say I didn't see the consequences. Once I started smoking, it drove a wedge between my closest friend, Ben, and me. Ben had drawn a red line between him and smoking. Drinking was okay, but smoking was on his list of nevers. And "never" meant something different to Ben than it did to me. So I began hiding it from him. I lied about what I was doing and who I was hanging out with on the weekends. Lying came easier than explaining my actions to my friend, and I didn't want the accountability. So I made new friends.

They were waiting for me on the bus. Friends who wouldn't judge me or look down on me for getting high. At that time, it felt like such a small sacrifice, walking away from a lifelong ally. It seemed somehow right, as if Ben was just one more person trying to hold me back under the guise of a false morality.

Mark was one of my new friends. Most mornings, he would sleep on the entire ride down to the city, wearing a hoodie and a hat that covered his face. His older brother happily smoked with us and took us to the head shop to buy bongs. I envied Mark, wishing my older brother, Pat, was as cool as his. He and his brother were so close, bonding over drugs without ever needing to hide the truth.

MAD

One week, when I was trying to get a handle on what was happening with Harry, I met for coffee with another mother whose son had gone through treatment. "They're bad kids," I said, describing Harry's new friends. "Abusing things and people around them without a care."

She brought me up short. "You think these boys are such a bad influence," she said. "Why would he hang with them? How do you know the other kids' parents aren't saying the exact same thing about Harry?" She was dead right. It had not occurred to me.

I often thought back to Harry's freshman year, watching him play on the football team. It's a sport I've never much liked. But I liked what it said about my son.

From the sidelines, you could see everything you needed to know about Harry. Buoyant, enthusiastic, and smiling that great smile, unfazed by the size difference between him and his teammates—one of whom we called the Refrigerator. Throughout the fall, PJ and I went to game after game and watched Harry suited up and beaming on the sidelines. He was rarely put in the game, and he certainly never touched the football, but his energy never waned.

During the last game of the year—I'm pretty sure it was nearly the last play of the game—PJ, Pat, and I were dumbfounded to see Harry run onto the field. Other parents hollered to us, "Watch Harry!" We scurried to the closest sideline, and there he was, bouncing like Ali in the ring. The quarterback handed him the ball, and he carried it, fleetingly, before being torn down to the ground by much larger players. Everyone cheered. Not because the run was long, but because they loved Harry.

It was a high point for Harry, being a member of that team. He hadn't asked for a thing, just a chance to be part of something bigger than himself, and the coach rewarded that soundness of spirit with a chance to run the ball.

It reminded me of something the boys' grade school coach had said about Pat, years earlier. "If I could put Harry's heart in Pat's body, that would be the ultimate athlete."

HARRY

After freshman year, I quit the football and wrestling teams. It was easy enough to justify. I stood five foot nothing and weighed 105 pounds, so the NFL wasn't exactly calling. Why waste all of that time practicing when instead I could be *living*?

The Prep had an interesting schedule. School ended at 2:15, but since so many kids had long commutes, the buses didn't leave until 5:20 each night. It saved parents from having to drive through rush hour traffic to pick them up. Three hours were set aside for extracurriculars: sports, homework, or in my case (having quit such obligations), getting high.

In North Philly, there was a huge park system: Fairmount. From a distance, it looked like a massive and beautiful green space, nestled between the concrete and brick. But as you got closer, you could see that it was riddled with litter and evidence of criminal activity. Fairmount was only a ten-minute ride from school, so my friends and I could smoke there after class and still make our way to the bus by 5:20. After some drops of Visine and the forty-minute cooldown on the bus, I would be sobered up and undetectable by the time I got home to my parents.

But it got to the point where those after-school highs weren't enough. I started sneaking out of our house at night. The first time I did it, I sat in my room for hours until I knew everyone would be in a deep sleep. Mark was waiting for me in a car just around the corner, but I made him sit for far longer than necessary, unwilling to risk my cover being blown by a creaky floorboard. My room was on the opposite side of the house from my parents, but the escape route ran past Pat's room, which was just as treacherous. As I crept downstairs and out the back door, I felt nervous but invigorated. I was free.

We parked just around the corner, where I could keep a watchful eye on my house, and smoked in Mark's car, looking for any sign of movement, or any lights turning on. But nothing happened. The house stayed dark long enough for us to smoke a blunt, and for me to make it safely back to my room with no one being the wiser.

When I got my driver's license a couple months later, a new step got added to my routine. I would put my parents' 1996 Chevy Suburban in neutral and push it down the hill, expending all the effort I had to get it rolling. I would climb into the car and wait until I'd rolled out of earshot before starting the engine. All of this so my family would not wake to find me and the car missing.

As my confidence grew, I snuck out more often and ventured farther from the house. I would go meet with my friends in various neighborhoods and sit in the car, smoking late into the night. Then I'd carefully return in time to get an hour or two of sleep before heading to school in the morning.

Occasionally, these exploits didn't go as planned. One Saturday night, I snuck out with a grand scheme in mind—driving the two hours to Atlantic City to smoke on the beach with four friends. It was spring, the night before Mother's Day, and the weather was starting to turn. On the drive to the shore, I thought about how fun it was to be sandwiched in the backseat with my friends, laughing, doing something risky. I'd never tried something like this before.

Then, at 3:22 A.M., the lights of a cop car illuminated our back window. They were pulling us over on a highway deep in New Jersey. As our car slowed to a stop, we let down the windows and watched the weed smoke billow out. I felt paralyzed. Surely we'd been caught. Yet, after a long stop that included a field sobriety test for the driver, the officer let us go. "I have kids your age and would hate to see them get in this much trouble on Mother's Day," he said.

Instead of counting our blessings at the cop's leniency, we laughed at how dumb the cop must have been and continued on to the shore, where we smoked a blunt on the beach. All went well, until we ran out of gas on the way back—right in the middle of I-95. By now the sun was coming up. The fear of my mom waking up and realizing I wasn't home began to course through my blood. We waited for AAA to bring us gas, and by the time they did, it was nearing eight.

When I finally made it home, I snuck back in the same way that I had left, going upstairs to my room. No one saw me. As I laid my head on the pillow and heard my parents beginning to stir, I laughed at my ridiculous luck.

There were consequences to this routine. My homework went unfinished, and my grades had started to slip. I showed up to school looking disheveled in my poorly fitting uniform of a shirt, tie, and blazer. My hair, long and shaggy. Things got harder with my parents, too. My mom, in particular, started grilling me. Where was I going? Who was I with?

When we fought, I would zero in on my eighteenth birthday, when I would no longer have to live under her roof. "I can't wait to move out!" I often yelled.

"I hope you don't mean that," she'd reply, her voice turning from anger to sadness.

Those moments gave me pause. I hated hurting my mom, but our worlds were so far apart. So I took the easy way out: I lied. I told her I was still hanging out with Ben. I knew she trusted him, maybe more than she trusted me. It was like a "get out of jail free" card, a way of trumping any lack of trust.

MAD

Years earlier, when our boys outgrew the family station wagon, we looked for a vehicle that could accommodate our bustling lives and love of road trips. I'm not one for minivans, so we took a leap: a gleaming white Chevrolet Suburban. Right out of the 1994 Tom Clancy movie *Clear and Present Danger*. It was a physical and financial stretch—a cavernous, high-riding vehicle that I quickly came to love. We could put everything in it, and it had lots of room for the boys, for Wally and Larry. We traveled tens of thousands of miles together in that car—to our house in Cape May, to South Carolina and Florida, carpooling to school, taking the boys to college campus visits.

A dozen years in, Harry got his driver's license and started driving the Suburban to get to and from the Prep, and our family SUV soon became the center of too many scenes in the action movie that was becoming Harry's life. Once, he told us, a guy jumped in through the open driver's side window while Harry was at a stop sign. The guy reached for the door handle to open the door from the inside, clearly trying to steal the car.

I didn't know it then, but he was using that car for other trips, too. Our white family Suburban had become the vehicle for Harry's descent. The whole time, I missed it.

It's the privilege. I was once a white suburban kid with lots of unearned advantages, and I knew it. Now Harry had even more, driving down Broad Street and claiming his education at a fancy prep school before returning to the white suburbs at night. Pain is universal, but the problems—the things we spend our anxiety on—are often different in the suburbs. I fretted over which great schools we would send our sons to, from grade school through high school and then into college. And of course there were the anxieties born of things other than privilege—our health, mental and physical, and the safety of our family.

As if we were surrounded by unseen airbags that would cushion the blow before any of our troubles got out of hand.

I was deceiving myself. I lived in that deceit for a long time.

HARRY

Everything seemed so manageable, so under control. After all the nights out, the smoking on the beach, whatever mess I brought upon myself—I prevailed. But one night during my junior year of high school, things changed.

It started as a day of heavy drinking in Fairmount Park. Typical. We started early, and it must have been noon when I blacked out. By the time I came to, it was nine in the evening, and I was lying naked on a bed in a North Philly row house. I went downstairs and discovered that the house belonged to my friend Mark's older brother. My friends Mark and Dave were there, along with Mark's older brother and two of his friends, all sitting on the couch playing NHL on Xbox.

With my head still spinning, I listened as Mark and Dave began telling me what had happened that afternoon. I always cringed at these stories, tales of the things I'd done with no recollection.

"You seriously don't remember anything?" they asked. "You made one hell of a scene. You passed out facedown in the field, then you threw up all over the fucking car! After that you kept begging to try our coke. So we let you."

At first, I had laughed at the insanity of what I was hearing. But the last detail stopped me. Cocaine was one of the last items left on my list of nevers. I couldn't believe it. What had I done? Sure, I'd been drinking heavily and smoking pot, but coke was a hard drug. It was another level, something for junkies and movie characters like Scarface.

"Are you serious?" I asked. "How much did I do? How does it feel?"

"There's still some left if you're so curious," Mark replied jokingly, cutting me off.

Without really thinking, I tried it again. Immediately, I felt more alive than ever. The drug took away the feeling of drunken grogginess, rejuvenating my senses. I was back in control: of my emotions, my fears, and my life. I took a couple more hits. Each time, the bitter taste on the back of my throat was followed by a euphoric rush that felt like rebirth. It was the epitome of living in the moment, with no anxiety or concern.

That night changed everything. I grew determined to incorporate drugs into every aspect of my life. I glorified them in every way—the feeling, the lifestyle, the inherent wrongness of it all. Coke was perfect. It left no smell, no stomach pain, and was easy to hide. It made the most trivial and mundane situations not only bearable, but thrilling. I loved the ritual of using: breaking it down into the finest possible powder, creating lines with my school ID card, then rolling a dollar bill into a perfect cylinder for snorting. I loved the way it stung, and then numbed, my sinuses. How it tasted bittersweet, like gasoline dripping down the back of my throat.

But it didn't take long before I realized doing coke in the bathroom off of a textbook or calculator between class periods wasn't as glamorous as I thought. And the $150-dollar-a-day habit was becoming a burden. So I decided to get a job at a local grocery store to help support my habit.

By now, school had become an afterthought. In my overconfident mind, I had no doubt that I would soon go to college and become rich enough to afford my habit. I just needed to wait until it all played out. I could see it so clearly. A fantasy in high definition. I would live in a big house with a beautiful wife and children, finally free from my parents' rules and supervision. I would spend my evenings on the porch, smoking a blunt and taking it all in. Reveling in a life well lived.

MAD

Fits and starts. I remember Harry puzzling over school and his future, trying to get something right. He was motivated to be independent, which meant being free of us. When it came time to look at colleges, he told us he wanted to go as far away as possible. He had always wanted to do daring things—stunt-riding bikes, skateboarding with kids too old for him.

One day, Harry came home and told me he'd gotten a job at Trader Joe's. He was unusually young to work there, but he applied and got it. The person who interviewed him was very complimentary. He said he'd never seen a kid Harry's age who was so smart or perceptive. And so, for a while, Harry worked hard at Trader Joe's.

Not surprising, he was well liked. One time, he left the store at the end of his shift to find our big white Suburban manically decorated by some young woman imploring him to go to the prom with her. When I shopped at his store, the manager or co-workers would stop me in the aisle and tell me how much they liked Harry, how much they admired his work ethic and charm.

That was always Harry: popular. I've often thought there was something about the name itself. Say the name *Harry,* and you can't help smiling.

Still, his work was a rare bright spot. In the months leading up to graduation, we fought endlessly. It happened when I found a lighter in his laundry, or prodded him about his grades or plans for the summer. It happened when he locked his car in the driveway and lingered by it for too long. When I brought it up, things would devolve quickly.

I tried to be reasonable. "Harry, I'm just trying to understand . . ." But one of us would blow our top in short order. Sometimes it was him. Sometimes it was me.

"You look terrible!" I would yell. "You're being selfish. There's no way you're telling me the truth!"

And Harry, always shooting back: "I can't wait until I'm eighteen! I'm moving out the second I turn eighteen! I hate it here!" Harry, in so many ways the heart of our family, could really lash out. But so could I.

Usually, PJ was caught between us—emotionally and physically. Normally, the two of us would retreat: Harry to the kitchen, me to the den. And PJ would be in the hall, standing physically between us as he tried to play peacemaker. But there was no peace to be made in those days.

I could hear him in the other room counseling Harry. "She's worried about you. She's trying to understand." Then he would come to me. "Mad, let it go. Give him some space. Do you know how mean you sound?"

The fights would typically end in stalemate. Sometimes, after a burst of anger, Harry would cry. At those points, I usually retreated into stoicism. My tears would come later—thinking over the fight, worrying about my son and the threat of losing him the moment he turned eighteen. Or sooner.

HARRY

Philly and its surrounding suburbs are a drug haven. Within an hour, you can go from farmland and trailer parks, through pristine suburbs, and into the chaos that is North Philly—all before ending up in the old historic city where the Founding Fathers made their promise of life, liberty, and the pursuit of happiness. As long as you have money, everything is within your reach.

Originally, I bought drugs from kids in the suburbs. It was easy, safe, and convenient. But as my craving grew, I found myself searching for a bigger, stronger fix in North Philly. Cutting out my prep school middleman and going straight to the source. It was exhilarating.

I would drive my parents' Suburban down Broad Street, glamorizing every step of the way. My couple hundred dollars of grocery store money felt like a fortune as I navigated the side streets to find my dealer. At the time, North Philly was experiencing a major spike in homicides, with an average of one murder per day. But I always felt safe. I looked down on my brothers and parents for leading such a sheltered existence.

I should make something crystal clear. My parents raised me with a strong sense of right and wrong. I knew doing drugs was wrong, and I knew where cocaine fell on the scale. But by now, I had suppressed that knowledge deep within me. No one close to me knew the extent of my using, and the risk of overdosing or being caught felt far away.

I felt invincible—and my encounters with cops helped solidify my confidence. More than once, I got pulled over with drugs in the car and talked my way out of being searched. Maybe it was looking younger than my years, the address on my ID, or the car that I drove. I know it had to do with the color of my skin. I skated past dozens of possible arrests. I passed field sobriety tests while high. One time, a cop pulled a bag of weed out of my pocket, only to give it back and send me on my way.

As I reached the end of high school, life looked good. I looked forward to getting high every day. I had a girlfriend, more friends than I could count, and more than ten acceptances to prestigious universities across the country—most of them accompanied by a scholarship. With each acceptance letter, my willingness to partici-pate in the pomp and circumstance of high school dwindled; I skipped class constantly; I refused to complete my assignments; and my drug use was getting more noticeable to everyone but me. Sure, I felt tired, even exhausted. But that was from sneaking out and lack of sleep, I reasoned.

My problems weren't the only ones in our house. Wally was dying. Mentally, he was as sharp as ever, but his body had started to fail. Between the radiation, visits with nurses and doctors, and trips to the hospital, there was plenty of distraction for me to hide behind.

Still, my mom and I battled. She was constantly finding things in my laundry. Lighters, condoms, stuff like that. Never actual drugs—I was too careful with those—but a pack of matches or an empty cigarette box was more than enough to set off a spark. I would arrive home to see the items laid out on my bed and my mom waiting for me. Or worse, I'd realize they were missing and start the countdown to our confrontation.

"It's just a lighter," I would say, disregarding her concern. It only frustrated her further.

"But why do you have it, what are you using it for?" She'd pry a little deeper, without directly acknowledging the truth. I was hurting my mom, and she was hurting me, but it wouldn't be for much longer. Once I moved out for college, things would improve.

With Mark and my other friends, I had found a new family. A chosen family that supported me in all of my choices, however destructive. We might not have been blood, but I felt a greater sense of loyalty to them than to anyone else. They knew all of my secrets, the things that would devastate my parents if they ever found out. My friends and I shared these things without fear of consequence. Together we protected one another's secrets at all cost.

MAD

I had taught at La Salle University since 2001, starting with two sections of Freshman Composition—English 107. At first, I worked as an adjunct, a J.D. in a sea of Ph.D.s. How would I ever fit in? But my department chairmen, Jim Butler and then Kevin Harty, always made me feel welcome and wanted. In meetings, Kevin said he was glad to have a lawyer on the faculty: "I never leave home without one."

I loved talking with the students about their writing. I wanted to share my love of words with them, just as my father had done with me. As the writer and professor William Zinsser said, "How we write is how we define ourselves." I marked the students' papers painstakingly with my red pen. After I had been teaching for a year or two, the chair of my department found me a full-time non-tenure-track position, and I expanded to teach business writing, legal writing, rhetoric, and ethics—even in the MBA program.

At home, Walter and Larry continued to live with us. In my eyes, Walter had always been cool in a way that most priests weren't, with his quick wit and his love of music and movies and Shakespeare. As a young man, he had been handsome, charismatic—and to me, he was still with it now at age eighty-two. He was weakened by illness but still able to enjoy life. Most Sundays, he said mass for us in our home. I loved those mornings in our living room, listening to Wally read from the Gospels—the boys and PJ, less so.

I have a favorite part of our Catholic mass. Just before communion, when the praying is almost complete, we say: "Lord, I am not worthy that you should come under my roof; only say the word and my soul shall be healed." I love that image, how it sums up my faith. Our sins and the cleansing of our sins. Humility and infinite possibility all at once. Years ago, after the Vatican II Council, the phrase was simplified to "Lord, I am not worthy to receive you," and I thought it a dumb modernization. I was pleased when the old image of Jesus coming under our roof returned. To this day, it makes me cry when I hear it and speak it aloud.

One weekend, Walter and Larry called from the house we shared in Cape May.

"Walter wanted me to call you," Larry said. "He's scared. He thinks there's blood in his urine."

"Is this the first time? How long have you been monitoring it?" I asked.

"It's news to me," Larry said. We agreed that he would keep monitoring it, and hung up.

He called back shortly thereafter. They had been eating beets all weekend, Larry said. It's probably nothing. I let the matter drift from my mind and returned to my work, marking papers. That is, until I got the third call.

"It's definitely not the beets," Larry said nervously. I drove to Cape May to bring them home.

Walter was diagnosed with bladder cancer, which really ticked me off. This good man had endured so much hardship and so much poor health. Now the thing that Walter most feared—cancer—had found him. Still, he bravely followed his treatment for months, cooperating with all the doctors' instructions. At one of his last radiation appointments, the doctor noted significant reductions in the tumors. But that news was short-lived.

Days later, Walter became gravely ill at our home. He woke up in the middle of the night, and suddenly he could not stand. Larry, PJ, and I sprang into action without waking the kids. I called 9-1-1, and when the ambulance arrived, PJ lifted Walter and carried him out of the house and into the dark. The cool but comforting light in the ambulance was haunting, and telling. I knew Walter was being driven away never to return.

HARRY

Those nights when I snuck out were the only times I could find peace. I could sit in a friend's car and smoke for hours—laughing, discussing everything, but nothing important. No one asked about my feelings or fears. We just smoked and reminisced about the good times, reaffirming that our decision to get high was the right one.

Late one night, as my friend brought me back to my family's house, I saw flashing lights. The police were in the driveway. I trembled as I checked my phone, looking for missed calls, texts—anything to show what had happened. Had my parents finally discovered my empty room? I froze in my seat as my friend drove past the house, the driveway lit with flashes of red and blue. I saw my mother stand-ing at the edge of the driveway, near the Suburban, with my dad at her side. They looked even more scared than me.

My friend dropped me off around the corner, and I snuck through a neighbor's property to our back door. As I walked through that first hallway, I ran into my dad. "What's going on?" I asked, pretend-ing to have just woken from all of the commotion. Mom walked in. She and dad told me Wally was sick and going to the hospital. Lost in the sadness and distraction, they didn't notice that I still had sneakers on.

I made my way back to my bedroom. As I lay down, I felt my heart pounding through my chest. The adrenaline and anxiety quickly broke into sadness. I had been so consumed with myself and my secrets, it never crossed my mind that the police could have been in my driveway for any other purpose. That their lights would shine across my parents' grief-stricken faces for anyone but me.

FOUR

TESTING
EACH OTHER

HARRY

As I sat chugging a sixteen-ounce bottle of white vinegar in my car—chasing it with a warm, flat Mountain Dew from under the seat—I started to sense that there might be a problem.

The fear of being caught only gets you so far. As my using increased, I eased off my cover-up. I neglected the eye drops and cologne and walked around campus with the unmistakable scent of weed emanating from my shirt. I took Xanax in class and completely blacked out a few times, only to hear stories of my recklessness and stupidity the following day.

One morning, I walked up to the entrance of school, late as usual and still trying to assemble my uniform as I trudged toward the steps. Distracted by the process of tucking in my shirt and slipping on a pretied tie, I failed to notice that someone was waiting for me. The dean of the school.

He stood tall, towering nearly a foot above me, his arms folded and a look on his face that said "Do not cross me." He was skilled at instilling fear in students.

"Come with me," he said, forcefully. I tried to convince him that I was late and needed to drop my bags in my homeroom class, but he wasn't having it. He told me to bring everything with me to his office.

With that, the soothing effects of the blunt I had just smoked disappeared. I felt red. What did he know? How did he know it? As we walked to his office, he wouldn't say. School had already started, so the hallways were empty. Everyone was sitting in class except for me.

When we arrived at the dean's office, he asked me directly, "Are you high right now?"

I don't know if I looked more shocked or high, but I immediately denied his claim. What was he talking about? How could he ever come to that outrageous conclusion?!

He searched my pockets, my school bag, and locker. When he came up empty-handed, I thought I was off scot-free. But then he decided to call my mom. The thought of her reaction scared me half to death. She would punish me in a way that the school never could: with the weight of her disappointment. I shrank at the thought of her shock and sadness.

I watched from across the desk as the dean slowly dialed the phone. We made eye contact, and a look of satisfaction filled his eyes when my mom answered. "Hello, Mrs. Cunnane, this is Mark, I have Harry in the office with me. We believe he is getting high at school." I couldn't hear the response, but knew it couldn't be good. I looked down at the floor.

He told her what was going on. He suspected I was high, and he wanted me to get a drug test—today. I panicked, scrolling mentally through the drugs that might show up in my system. When was the last time I used cocaine, or Xanax?

After a long day of sitting in the dean's office, a purgatory of sorts, I was told to drive to meet my mom at La Salle. From there, we would go together to Quest Diagnostics for a drug test.

I failed that first test, and in the two months since, had done the same with each of the tests that my mom administered at home.

When she tested me, my mom would hide in the bathroom, carefully opening the box containing a small cup and a series of strips to test urine for various substances. Marijuana, cocaine, ecstasy, heroin, meth, and more. Then she would call me into the bathroom to complete my part. When I finished peeing in the cup—with my dad standing by to make sure I didn't tamper with the results—my mom would lock herself in the bathroom alone and wait for the results to appear. I would plead with her to open the door—to throw away the test and let me talk to her. Lies flowed from my mouth. Although what I really felt was sadness, I showed only anger toward my mother. I blamed her for putting me in this situation. *How can you be doing this? What kind of parent drug-tests their kid?*

Each time the two lines appeared on the drug test—signaling positive for drug use—the look of sadness on her face was enough to make me cry. My only consolation was that the tests had only showed pot. It wasn't the result she wanted, but the full scope of my use—my real secret—would live another day.

MAD

I guess I drug-tested Harry a half a dozen times over the years. The pattern in our house was always the same, as predictable as the tides: As our fighting rose over the course of a week, I would look online for home test kits, feeling completely inept. Where to buy and send them? Were they reliable? What did they screen for? And how did you get the results back? Then, when my anger boiled over, I would force a test.

Later, I realized that the escalating temperature in the house gave Harry time to prepare, to attempt to clean his system beforehand. Harry and I were a pair of well-matched idiots, he trying to fool me, me trying to outwit him, both of us failing in the end.

And PJ was not in the dark. He, too, was worried, but he was not in favor of testing Harry. It came back to trust—love and trust for his boys. But I didn't give a damn about boosting Harry's trust in me. I wanted the truth. I wanted peace. I wanted Harry back.

The tests always took place in our first-floor powder room. A small half-bath on the first floor, under the stairs, as close to public as it gets in our house. In fact, I would insist that PJ go into the room with Harry to be sure he was the one filling the cup. I stood by and made sure the door remained ajar.

On one of the first of these occasions, I remember there being a negotiation: Harry kept talking with PJ in some faraway room, explaining there was no reason to test, on and on. Finally, PJ came to me. "Harry said he'll take it, but he admitted the test will be positive for pot." I was unsympathetic and sent the urine sample off just the same. Days later, the results came back, positive for pot but otherwise muddy. No clarity on anything else.

Maybe I should have been relieved it was only pot. Plenty of people in my life had smoked it—PJ included, before I met him. But I wasn't relieved. And I didn't buy it. Others could go through that phase, but not my own kid. The one whose precious hands I felt slipping away from me. From himself and his beautiful gifts.

HARRY

I searched Google and tried all of the old wives' tales that people say help you pass, from downing detox drinks to taking enough niacin pills to turn your skin bright red and leave it itching and burning for days. None of my friends had clean urine, so borrowing it from them wasn't an option. I didn't know what to do. Each time, I would go home and fail another test. I dreaded the impending scene: me being exposed in the bathroom under the stairs in our hallway yet again.

I could usually sense when the tests were coming. My mom and I would start by battling over little things. A messy room or a dirty car, maybe. Pressure would build to a point where everyone in my family could feel it. Inevitably, she would reach her breaking point and pull a drug test kit from the hallway closet.

These were the first times that I sincerely tried to stop using. I would sense the test coming—the tension building—and try with all the willpower I could muster to take even just a few days off. But I couldn't. I could stop using pills and coke, but pot was a different story. Always, I would keep getting high. Right up until I had to take and fail another test.

As the deadline for picking a college neared, I thought about quitting altogether. But I was afraid to tell my friends that I was even considering such a thing. After all, we still glamorized getting high, and we never talked about the consequences. As we sat in cars late at night, getting high, I would tell my buddies: "My parents are so wrong. If they knew the benefits of getting high, they would too. Hell, everyone would."

But that was another lie. Inside, I was plotting a change. I had decided that college would be a fresh start. I would study at the College of Charleston in South Carolina, a school that none of my friends was planning to attend. It made so much sense. In Charleston, I wouldn't know where to find hard drugs, and I would fall back squarely in the bounds of societal norms: drinking, sure, and maybe occasionally smoking pot. But no more pills. No more coke. I would get through the summer. Then I would leave for college and start over with a clean slate.

MAD

Harry's final year of high school was marked by many things. Losing his enthusiasm for the job at Trader Joe's. Sneaking around and locking the cars he drove. Going out back to smoke and skulk. Fighting constantly with me.

And there was something missing, as I look back. Ever since that night of underage drinking, when his friends were arrested and Harry ran into the Acme, he had never shown up drunk or high at home.

Around the house, Harry's eyes were bloodshot, and his affect was becoming flatter and flatter. With the flatness came poor eye contact and limited conversation. As soon as he came home at the end of a day, he would say he had somewhere to go—either to take a desperately needed nap, or just to go out, with Mark or one of his other new friends. More than living *in* our house, Harry mostly lurked around it, leaving a cloud of too much cologne in his wake. Smoking was part of the excuse, but it didn't explain everything.

I remember a day when our dearest friend and next door neighbor, Sean—the kind of neighbor who walks through your front door without a knock and wanders into the kitchen to grab a Diet Coke—pointed to Harry smoking on our front stoop. "Mad, Harry just looks lousy," he said. "Charlotte's worried it's drugs."

In that moment, I was offended. It hurt to know that Sean and Charlotte were thinking it too. So I brushed him off, while feeling wounded on the inside. "Oh, God, they think my kid's a drug addict." My worst fears were reflected in Sean's eyes, my lighthearted neighbor who cared deeply for us, especially for Harry.

Looking back, I'm sad about that reaction. Why did the truth offend me? Did I think we were too good for it? Damn the stigma. Damn my ignorance.

As Harry prepared for college, I felt anxious about the future. We needed to get him away from the dysfunction of his current life and friends. So when Harry told us he had decided on the College of Charleston, it came as the most pleasant surprise.

We had traveled to Charleston with the boys many times. PJ's favorite uncle, Frank, lived there, and we visited him every year by car or plane. Frank and his wife, Ditty, considered PJ their own son. In their humble Southern home, you could count on constant streams of delicious food—the best fried chicken—and talk. We spent countless hours chatting with them on their front porch.

And so we were elated when Harry chose Charleston. We hadn't pushed him there in the way I had tried to push our eldest to Georgetown three years earlier. I knew this was Harry's choice to make—and to my mind, he had made the right one.

But some things did not feel right. And we had a summer to get through first.

HARRY

In the summer of 2008, we rented a house in Ocean City, New Jersey, me and a few of my closest drug-using buddies. No parents, no rules, no expectations. I saw it as one last summer of fun, a final chance to live it up with the friends I would soon leave behind.

My mom wasn't so excited. I had pleaded with her for months to let me go. "It's tradition, everyone does it!" I kept telling her. I was wearing her down, saying the same thing over and over, waiting for her to cave. Maybe it would be easier for her if I weren't around to argue with all summer. Maybe her friends, who were allowing their kids to spend the summer away from home, convinced her. None of it mattered. All I cared about was getting my first taste of freedom. To my surprise, I got it.

Within days after we moved in, our place in Ocean City devolved into a complete shithole. Empty bottles and roaches from blunts littered every surface, from the floors to the coffee table and nightstand. At one point, the toilet stopped working and was backed up to the brim with feces, so we had to walk a few blocks to the boardwalk just to go to the bathroom. Still, I loved every second of it. The aesthetics didn't matter; all I cared about was having the freedom to wake up and get high or drunk and spend every second of the day that way. I was seventeen years old, still a child emotionally, but convinced I was living like a man. No matter how unsustainable it was, I wanted that summer to last forever.

I lived on the pullout sofa on the first floor of the modest three-bedroom duplex. We kept our curtains drawn—from the porch, there was no indication of the chaos that lay within. Our home was a lot like me. Somewhat put together on the surface, but riddled with secrets below.

MAD

I saw zero value in Harry spending the summer in Ocean City. Look how badly high school was ending. The kids he planned to live with—his new friends—had equally lousy records. And besides, our family already had a house at the shore. Why not get a job in Cape May and live there?

Somehow, I lost that fight too. Harry headed to the shore and moved into a small apartment for the summer.

The reports from Ocean City weren't promising. A few weeks in, he had no job, no money, no direction, no remorse for the hell he'd put us through in his final months at the Prep. Harry told one tale after another of problems at the apartment: a break-in, stuff stolen, citations from the landlord. I wondered how long the owner—who allegedly lived upstairs—would stand these losers. Even at my distance, twenty miles down the Garden State Parkway, I could not.

One day, I drove to Ocean City for a check-in. A surprise. When I pulled up to the apartment, Harry wasn't there—nobody was—but the front porch foretold the story. Ashtrays, beer cans, broken chairs, and a state of general slop. The door was unlocked, so I went in. There were the classic mattresses on the floor, filth everywhere, a kitchen in decay. But what caught my eye was the bag of pot—and who knows what else—that I found in one bedroom. Furious, I stomped over to the stain-smeared bathroom and flushed the stash down the toilet. "I hope that makes them mad," I thought, "because I sure am."

Outside, I called my son. "Harry, I just visited your shithole! I'm on the front porch. Come back here now to get your things, you're finished." Harry did not have a defense. I guess I still had some say with him.

As Harry drove back to the apartment, a couple of his so-called friends showed up. They feigned a "Hello, Mrs. Cunnane," but I was in no mood. I'm not one to curse, or at least I wasn't before that day. But I might as well have been in the Navy that day. "Get your shit in the car," I snapped when Harry arrived. "I don't want to hear one goddamn excuse."

No doubt, Harry was embarrassed. Here was his forty-nine-year-old mother coming to yank him from his bachelor pad in front of his friends. But I didn't care. In fact, I wanted to embarrass him—not to hurt him permanently, but to demonstrate that he and his loser friends hadn't fooled me. Looking back, I'm sure they didn't give a damn. But in the moment, I felt I had won this simmering summerlong battle. I had controlled the moment and liberated Harry from a bad place.

Harry shoved his belongings into black trash bags and threw them in the back of our Suburban. We drove home in silence, both of us clearly steamed. We were losing our grip. Mine, on what was happening to the happy, thriving boy I had known. His, on his own life.

But I had shown Harry something that day: What he constantly claimed was an okay scene was anything but. He just never thought I'd come looking.

HARRY

A few days after my eighteenth birthday, I got my first tattoo. I had thought about the design for months before settling on an image that would remind me of that summer: a cross topped with a crown, and a banner with the words LIVE TODAY, DIE TOMORROW draped over it. It was another firm decision that I made "like a man"—while planning to hide it from my mom for the rest of my life. I knew exactly how she felt about tattoos.

The design really spoke to my feelings at the time, with the cross representing all of the pain I was going through, and the crown projecting an overly optimistic belief that I would always come out on top. The motto on the banner was a reminder that I truly didn't care if I made it to my twenty-fifth birthday alive, so long as I could get high today. (Of course, when my mom inevitably found out about the tattoo, I gave a different, less grim spin on its meaning.)

Mark took me to a tattoo shop he knew about in Kensington, a neighborhood in North Philly. It was my first time seeing that part of the city. Most people from the suburbs would have been repulsed. It's a drug mecca, filled with junkies and dealers conducting business out in the open. I loved every second of it. I can still hear the rumbling of the El train overhead, mixed with the constant sirens from police cars and ambulances. I can still feel that chaos. It was nothing like the suburbs where I grew up, but I felt more comfortable smoking a Newport under the El than I did in my own bedroom.

As summer came to an end, I prepared myself for the move to Charleston with a renewed belief that I would start fresh, stop using hard drugs, and become the success I always envisioned. Sure I was having fun, the most I'd ever had, but I knew it wasn't sustainable. The drug tests, the disappointment, the lack of structure. If I wanted to live on my own, without the expectations of my parents,

I needed to hold a job, I needed to be self-sufficient. I would have to graduate from college and prepare myself for the real world. Most of all, I needed to prove to myself that I could do it.

To prepare, I did all of the usual back-to-school shopping. Trips to Bed Bath & Beyond and Target, working with my parents to pick out the twin-sized bedding, trash cans, and everything else I would need for freshman year. It felt exciting. I could picture my time at school: four years filled with partying and new friends and concluding in graduation.

During the tour for prospective students, the guide showed us the beautiful courtyard that hosted graduation each spring. At the Charleston commencement ceremony, there would be no caps and gowns. The men would wear white tuxedo jackets, just as I had done at my high school. Here the oaks were draped in Spanish moss. I could see all of us there—my parents and brothers and family—celebrating me for once.

MAD

I was so hopeful. Hopeful that Charleston would save him. How I wanted Harry to find friends there—new friends, gentle Southern friends.

We all traveled to Charleston, staying in our favorite hotel and nervously completing family-freshman orientation. It felt similar to the weekend three years earlier when we had taken Pat to the University of Miami—but this time the nervousness was different. Whereas Pat had needed us, needed me, for all the shopping and setup of his dorm, Harry seemed less interested in help. He just went with PJ to the Bed Bath & Beyond in Charleston and handled it mostly on his own. He asked us to skip orientations. "I don't need it, I'm cool." It seemed he barely wanted me to see his new room. We were not needed. See you later.

So we left town, saddled not with confidence but with worry.

Harry had gotten what he wanted, a life free from his parents. Now, what on earth would he do with it?

HARRY

Within hours of my parents dropping me off, my roommate mentioned that he had some weed. "Do you smoke?" he asked. A couple minutes later, we were lighting up in the dorm's bathroom. As I stood there getting high, I knew it wouldn't be enough. I knew I would need a stronger fix.

A switch had flipped. Before my head hit the pillow that first night of college, my dreams of a fresh start were long gone.

MAD

How did that semester go? I never really knew. Harry didn't say much, only that he never felt like he fit in. The place felt cliquey, he said. Too Southern, too white. On top of that, his roommate was not working out—though we weren't clear why. Pat and Harry were so different: Pat called us every day, a too-tall kid who got teary-eyed when he expressed his worry; Harry, smaller, more stoic, hiding his.

PJ and I felt sad for this kid who had wanted Charleston, the kid with so many gifts. Harry, to us, was a beaming human being. A kid with big, beautiful eyes that matched his huge heart. That's what I always saw in Harry: his big heart. A heart with so many chambers, but somehow now lost.

When Harry came home for Thanksgiving break, he talked about how unhappy he was. "Mom, I don't want to be there anymore." I was disappointed. It felt like Harry didn't get it— did not recognize or appreciate the education in front of him.

So PJ and I planned a time to talk with Harry alone. A come-to-Jesus meeting. We had just learned from a good source— Pat—that Harry had followed through on the tattoo he was threatening to get during the summer. Pat had seen Harry boasting about it on Facebook. That might explain why Harry, after being yanked out of the Ocean City house, never went to the beach with us, never went without a T-shirt in the August sun of Cape May.

And so, in the darkened bar of our house, PJ and I sat Harry down and talked over all sorts of troubling stuff. "I'm worried about you, Harry," I told him. "You *wanted* to go to Charleston. You were excited about it." How had things gone so wrong in a matter of one semester?

Harry didn't divulge much. "It's just not for me," he said.

I wanted to see his grades. "They're good," he deflected, and gave us a thin summary of his grades. But he refused to sign the release allowing me to see them.

So we moved on from the issue of college and fell into a familiar argument: his habits at home. "Here you are, back only a couple of days—and as usual, you're not hanging with us," I said. "You're out, God knows where, with the same kids who dragged you down through the Prep."

"You don't even know them!" he said. Ever loyal, he defended his friends, and the two of us were back at square one. All the same sounds, and strains, and stress were back. It felt as though he'd never left for college.

And yet I had planned an ending for the conversation that would cut through the tension. A joke—or so I thought.

On my right foot, I had drawn a faux tattoo in blue Bic ink: *delasalle,* a reference to St. Jean-Baptiste de La Salle, the patron saint of teachers and the namesake of my university. As our tense meeting came to an end, I closed by telling Harry that his father and I knew about his tattoo. Would he please show it to us?

Harry looked baffled. "How did you know?" he asked.

I said to Harry, "You show me yours, and I'll show you mine." Puzzled, Harry removed his shirt as I removed my sock. His tattoo was the size of small baseball mitt on his right flank, with an ominous saying, something about "live today, die tomorrow." Mine, a little Bic-inked signature.

But the stunt did not go as planned. I was sure Harry would see through the cheap ink and realize how ridiculous his own tattoo looked, but he didn't. Harry believed that mine was real. I stared at PJ in disbelief, begging silently for help.

Harry questioned me. "Where did you get it?" Trying to play out the nonsense, I said: "Oh, a charming little place in Bucks County." "What'd they charge you?" I had no idea, so I said $400. Harry couldn't believe it. He said I'd been robbed. "Mom, nine little letters, are you kidding me?"

Yes, I was—trying in my own lame way to make a connection with my son. But the whole thing got ahead of me. Harry ran out of our house laughing. Oh, dear God. Out he went, texting and calling Charlotte and his other friends: "I never saw this coming: my middle-aged mom has a tattoo!!!"

HARRY

When I told my mom I'd gotten good grades, that wasn't a lie. College was easy enough that I could show up only on test days and skip all the lectures without penalty. Test taking came naturally to me, so I never felt that I had to study.

The trouble came when I wasn't in class. In Charleston, I met people who could smoke without destroying their lives. People who made me feel welcome. People who cared about me. Some of the nicest, most authentic and genuine people I've ever encountered. But when I hung out with them, I grew fearful of showing them how strong my obsession was with drugs. I worried that if anyone really got to know me, they would leave.

By the end of my first semester, the fear got the best of me. I decided to trade this beautiful city for the comfort I knew at home. I would go back to Philly, to La Salle University, where my mom had taught for years. That was the deal. So I packed all of my belongings into the back of a Ford Explorer and headed home. When my transcript showed up for the transfer, the 3.75 GPA was enough to buy me some goodwill and freedom from my parents.

Back in Philly, at La Salle, I felt instantly comfortable. I was back living in a dorm in North Philly, within minutes of my old dealers and friends. I fell into a group of people that reminded me of home—not Jenkintown home, but Kensington home. Drugs were everywhere. When you walked down the main avenue, people would offer you heroin, crack, coke, pills, subs, and more.

The only challenge was avoiding my mom on campus. I didn't want her to see me smoking a cigarette, let alone getting high or drunk before lunchtime. But on the bright side, when I was able to get myself together, I could track her down and ask for money.

MAD

Harry and I were back together, in our dance of rivals. How ridiculous—or maybe not, as I look back. We had no reason to be face-to-face, back in our contentious dance, but there we were, on the same campus. Me seeing one side of Philadelphia, him seeing the other.

As I taught at La Salle, Harry got into trouble.

HARRY

One afternoon, a friend asked if I would go for a drive with him to Norristown, a not-quite-suburb forty-five minutes outside Philadelphia. He was buying pills from a guy who worked in the school cafeteria. "If you come with me, I'll give you some," he said.

When we got to Norristown, we pulled onto a small side street lined with row homes. After a brief wait, an older man emerged from one of the houses and got into the backseat of my friend's pickup truck. He started telling us about his wife. She was dying of cancer. She didn't have much time left, and she hated the way the pills made her feel. "We can't afford her cancer treatments," he said at one point. "I'm just trying to make ends meet."

He sold us her entire prescription of thirty-milligram Percocet. Not knowing what they were worth, he practically gave them away. In a distorted way, it felt as if we were helping him, like our money was going toward a good cause. But the part of me that empathized with the man with the dying wife was quickly overruled by the side that saw an easy score—a great deal on solid drugs.

When the man exited the truck, my friend offered me a couple of the pills. Percs had never been my thing, but I wasn't one to turn down free drugs. I crushed one of the pills and quickly snorted it off the owner's manual in his car.

Within minutes, I felt a high that trumped anything that I had ever experienced. My body tingled. My mind slowed, homing in on the pleasure and blocking out any anxiety. I could feel my breath and my heartbeat, a pulsing euphoria. It was like the euphoria of cocaine without the anxiety, the mental numbness of alcohol without the lack of control, the relaxation of weed without the paranoia. It gave me everything I wanted without a side effect in sight.

As we drove down the highway, my desire for alcohol, weed, coke, ecstasy, and everything else flew right out the pickup truck's window.

I fell in love with pills.

FIVE

A SMALL BLUE PILL

HARRY

A small blue pill. That's all it took. For the first weeks and months, those pills made me feel like I had superpowers. I enjoyed more energy, more focus, and more peace than ever before.

Life changed at a rapid pace. The obsession to find and use more and more Percocet overwhelmed me. I became unwilling to spend my money on anything other than pills, including food. At first, I delayed eating because I didn't want to dilute the high. Then those hourlong delays turned into days—until soon I hardly ate at all. My tolerance was growing, too. What started as a $20-a-day habit quickly turned to $100, then $200.

Drugs were all I had money for. I craved cigarettes obsessively, but even they came after pills on my mental shopping list. The local Chinese restaurant sold "loosies," single Newport 100s, for fifty cents, so I would collect change and cash in whenever possible. Once, when my roommate's coin jar had been raided of anything silver, I counted out fifty pennies and walked down to the store, only to be turned away. "We don't take pennies," the woman behind the counter said with a sense of satisfaction. I went out to the corner and stood there until I could persuade a passerby to give me a cigarette. Then it was back to the bigger picture. Finding at least $20 so I could cop another pill.

The only time I worried about eating was when my migraines became so unbearable that even a couple hundred milligrams of opioids wouldn't help. In those moments, I would search the local gas station for food. My goal: finding the cheapest item with the highest calorie count. I found it in Tastykake brand Coconut Juniors, a one-dollar snack that gave you 380 calories and enough sugar to kill a migraine. Most mornings, I woke with an extreme burning sensation in my gut. My body was trying desperately to evacuate the burning hot bile and stomach acid that was rotting me from the inside out. As soon as I came to, I would run to the bathroom and throw up. Then I was safe to start using again without the risk of losing any of my hard-earned fix.

When I stayed at home, my room was located as far away as possible from my parents', my mom noticed the vomiting and quickly became desperate to find the cause. "What's going on? What do you think it is?" she would often ask. I needed an excuse, something that would explain my vomiting, terrible teeth, and emaciated appearance. I remembered that I had been sick as a young child, constantly throwing up. So when my mom wondered out loud if this was a recurrence of that earlier episode, I let her believe it.

My mom and I went together to doctor after doctor, seeing the top specialists in the area. I underwent testing and endoscopies, always worried that the endoscopy would reveal the telltale blue powder in my esophagus and stomach. For some reason, I was never concerned enough to warn the anesthesiologist that I was on "medication" before they put me to sleep.

After dozens of appointments, I was finally given a diagnosis. Eosinophilic esophagitis, or "EoE," as the doctors called it. They explained that it's an inflammation of the esophagus, often a result of an allergy, with two common symptoms: choking and excessive vomiting. To confirm the theory, they suggested one more set of testing with an allergist.

As we walked into the allergist's office, I felt relieved. Maybe my mom would be less worried about my drug use and more focused on finding a cure for my newfound condition. We made small talk with the nurse as she scratched my back with dozens of common allergens, trying to pinpoint what might be causing my flare-ups.

After a while, the nurse gave me shots with the concentrated doses of the same allergens. She left the room and let us know that the doctor would be back in shortly.

"How are your classes going?" my mom asked, changing the subject while we waited.

"Great," I lied, not wanting to open that door. By now, I avoided details like the plague, not letting anyone get close enough to inspect the cover I'd carefully constructed.

Between uncomfortable silences, we ignored the elephant in the room—that there was more to the story of my sickness, and we both knew I'd never tell her. We had grown so far apart, I was no longer capable of being honest with my mom. I could see the hope in her eyes that this doctor's visit might help us find the real answer, accompanied by the fear that the cause might be exactly what I knew it to be.

MAD

During intake, a nurse asked Harry if he had any medications in his system, warning that it was dangerous to undergo testing if he had taken anything. He claimed no, nothing. "All right, then," the nurse said. "Let's go back."

I remember being in the room with Harry as the doctor and nurse did a series of pinpricks on Harry's back, rows of them, to see if there was any reaction to grass, pet dander, foods, or dozens of other potential culprits. I sat there worrying as Harry, shirtless, held on to his left pants pocket. He was hiding something, and yet I didn't ask in that moment what he was holding on to.

The first round of sticks tested mildly positive for grass and trees and some nuts. But nothing that the doctor thought abnormal. The nurse administered a second round of tests—introducing bigger doses of the allergens that hadn't gotten a reaction from Harry.

And then something went wrong. All of a sudden, as Harry and I sat alone in the exam room waiting for the second set of results to develop, I saw Harry turn pale, gray-white and clammy. He appeared to pass out. His blood pressure was dropping, and he gripped his left pocket tightly as I laid him back on the exam table and yelled for help.

HARRY

My lips started to tickle, then my tongue. A moment later, my throat felt like it was starting to collapse. I told my mom what was happening, and she immediately ran for the doctor. He flew into the room and, after taking one look at me, announced that he would be administering a shot of epinephrine. "He's going into anaphylactic shock," he said. My throat would completely close within minutes.

The shot worked, for a few minutes at least. But it wasn't long before the reaction started happening again. The epinephrine wasn't enough to stop it. After multiple shots of adrenaline, my throat kept closing. All I could think about were the contents of my pocket—a small cellophane bag filled with Percocets. Nothing else, not even death, had the opportunity to enter my mind. I was consumed by the fight-or-flight instinct. Knowing I couldn't flee, I fought to stay awake. I had to protect my secret.

MAD

When Harry stabilized, the doctor explained that this was a very rare reaction. "Mrs. Cunnane, in all my years of practice, I've never seen that happen before." Maybe the test samples had been too much for Harry's system, he said, or maybe they were the wrong samples. Harry wondered if the nurse might have screwed up the test and sent him into shock.

We were all afraid, and I took no comfort from the medical team. They looked confused, squinting skeptically, as though there was some factor they had missed. In their eyes I saw a combination of trying to decide whether they had done something wrong—or we had. It's never a good feeling when the doctor looks as puzzled as the mother following a routine test.

Now I was determined: We were going to the ER. This was my backstop. The hospital would draw his blood, and the truth would be revealed. The ultimate test that I couldn't administer at home.

We sat there for a long while, arguing—Harry determined to get out and go home, and me determined to go to the hospital. Harry fought hard, but I was having none of it. In the end, Harry left the allergist's office in an ambulance, headed to the hospital.

I followed in my car, staring in through the glass in the rear of the ambulance. Scared and searching and angry. But as we got closer to the hospital, I thought back to the moment before Harry went into shock, when we were waiting for the tests to develop. What had he been clutching in his left hip pocket?

HARRY

Over and over my mom and the doctor asked me if I had taken any medication. Was there anything I wasn't telling them? Anything at all that might have caused this adverse reaction? Time and time again, I said no. I lied. Even as I held on tight to the small cellophane bag that held the truth.

Even when my throat was closing—when I didn't know if I would make it out alive—it never crossed my mind that I should tell the doctors about the Percs. I would rather suffocate than tell my mom my secret. My death would be easier for her to take than knowing the truth. Having run out of options, the doctor agreed to call 9-1-1.

A few minutes later, paramedics came through the front doors of the office, wheeling a gurney. "Sir, we need you to lie down so we can get you to the hospital," they said.

"Hold on," I told them, impatiently. "I've got to go to the bathroom first, I'll be right out." They reluctantly let me go.

With the bathroom door locked behind me, I snapped into action. I swallowed one of the pills from the bag. Then, with great reluctance, I flushed the rest, watching each twenty-dollar pill disintegrate as it circled the bowl. The cellophane wouldn't flush, so I grabbed it from the water, wrapped it in toilet paper, and buried it deep inside the trash can.

In the ambulance, the paramedics started taking my vital signs, asking me what had happened. "Do you have any known allergies?" "Are you taking any medications?" I pled ignorance to every question. Watching my mom's car following close behind the ambulance, I felt safer knowing she couldn't hear this interrogation.

They hooked me up to an IV and began administering Benadryl immediately. I watched intently as they took notes and assessed the situation. Then, for the first time since the incident began, I felt a fresh wave of fear when one of the paramedics started drawing my blood through the IV line. I watched as they prepared three small vials of my blood, placing labels on them and covering each one with a different-colored cap. I became completely fixated, knowing that within those canisters, the confirmation of all my mom's fears was sloshing around. This was it. An indisputable piece of evidence that would show exactly which drugs were in my system.

At the hospital, they placed the vials into a yellow bin attached to the gurney. I watched that bin intently as the paramedics wheeled me into the room. I had to get rid of the blood, but with doctors and my mom watching, there was no opportunity for me to make a move.

Then a chance came. The doctor left the room, giving me a moment of privacy to remove my clothes and replace them with a hospital gown. I snuck the vials under the gown, tucked them between my legs, and shuffled to another bathroom unauthorized, moving carefully to avoid letting anything fall to the floor. Inside, I shattered the vials in the sink and rinsed the blood down the drain. Last, I removed the label with my name and carefully placed it in the needle disposal box along with the shards of glass. The box was the only spot I knew no one would stick their hands into, even if they knew what was inside.

And just like that, the fear was gone. I still had to get through the hospital visit, but now I knew no one would discover the truth unless I told it to them. My secret was safe to live another day.

MAD

Why didn't I challenge Harry right there in the doctor's office?

There were lots of reasons. One I immediately seized on was that we were headed to the ER, and professionals would soon test Harry's blood. And there were other reasons that weren't clear to me in the moment. I wanted to trust Harry. I did not want to shame him. And by that point, I was too angry to ask and truly listen. To this day, I'm not sure why I didn't challenge him more directly. What was he holding on to? What was I holding on to?

The truth, I now realize, is harder to admit. Maybe I was embarrassed. Maybe I did not really want to know. And most of all, I thought I had him—and the ultimate drug test administered in the hospital.

But I did ask the doctors one last question as we were leaving the ER. "How about his blood? What did the tests show?"

"All clear," they said. We were dismissed.

HARRY

When we got home from the hospital, my high quickly wore off. I had flushed all of my drugs. Now I had to get more, and somehow do it with my mom understandably keeping a closer eye on me.

Back at La Salle, things got worse as I was introduced to the pains of withdrawal. Where the Percocets once gave me a feeling of energy and focus, that feeling was now fading, replaced with constant lethargy. I woke up sick each morning, and the vomiting no longer made me feel better. The only cure was to take more pills.

My grades were abysmal. I put in zero effort, hardly ever showed up to class, and found myself a frequent visitor to the university's judiciary board. Whether I was there for allegations that I had slashed someone's tires or gotten into a fight, it felt like I couldn't catch a break. To the school, I was the boy who cried wolf. I denied my wrongdoing time and time again. "Hearsay! With malicious intent!" I'd cry. But the administration saw through it.

Each time, my mother would stand by my side, vouching for me. She was my superpower in these hearings. As a professor at the school, her word carried more weight than many of the student witnesses'. And undoubtedly more than mine.

MAD

The circumstances weren't ideal, but I was happy to have Harry on campus with me. I wanted him to have space, and the fact that I taught under my maiden name, Professor Dean, gave him distance if he wanted it. Maybe he would spend time at La Salle and see what a great place it was. Maybe he'd appreciate how his mom's hard work earned him a shot at a good, tuition-free education—if only he would claim it.

But Harry lacked maturity. His emotional growth seemed arrested some years back—the little boy not willing to grow up—except now he was no longer a little boy, and the act was growing unattractive. At La Salle, he oscillated between doing well and causing the wrong kind of stir. I remember one of my colleagues in the English Department telling me that Harry wrote well and argued his points "like a lawyer." But that was one of the few times a professor sang Harry's praises. More often, he was getting in trouble.

I heard the rumors, but I could never bring myself to believe them. Families fall into patterns, and I had fallen into a pattern of my own: the warrior mother who tries to pull the truth out of her son, while standing in defense of him in public.

Don't get me wrong. I knew Harry was a problem—at home and on campus. I just didn't think he was the only problem. I tried to be by his side, to defend him—to protect him. But the stakes were higher now than when I had defended his long hair in grade school. And I knew I couldn't protect him forever.

HARRY

I had a dorm room, but I never stayed there. I hated having to walk past the security guards, my entry and exit monitored by the swipe of a student ID. So I crashed most nights at my buddy Zach's row house, only a block from campus. In the morning, I would wake up in withdrawal and usually decide to skip class.

I grew paranoid that people were following me. The staff, other students, random strangers. I had been bringing drug dealers into frat parties, to the frustration of my classmates, and making a total fool of myself while I was there. No one wanted to tolerate my antics—and one night, I found myself face-to-face with the consequences of putting myself at odds with pretty much the whole campus.

Around two in the morning, I was in a frat house, smoking on the couch. I had been blacked out for hours, having snorted Xanax around noon and started to drink by three. Word got out that I was there, and some of the frat boys made their way home.

When they burst through the door, I knew what was coming. I made a run for a back door, but they cornered me in the kitchen. There was no way out. I ducked and tried to cover my face, knowing I was outnumbered and didn't stand a chance in this fight. I took a right hook to the stomach and bent down in pain. Then a kick from a Timberland boot landed square on my eye. The beating continued until it was crystal clear I had lost.

I stumbled out of the house and walked toward my home on Eighteenth Street, three blocks away. I was shirtless, bleeding from my eye. I couldn't see myself, but I knew it was bad.

Halfway home, the lights from a police cruiser illuminated the sidewalk. They dragged me into the car and drove me back to the frat house, then handcuffed me and threw me into the back of another patrol car. I was shocked—and comforted—to see one of my close friends, Chris, already in the backseat.

"Damn, you got fucked up," he said, smiling.

Chris explained that he'd heard what happened and run out to get revenge for me, but the cops picked him up on the way. We laughed as he told me the story.

Through the patrol car's window, I could hear the frat guys telling the cops that I'd broken into their house and that they'd fought back in self-defense. I screamed in protest—but honestly, I didn't know the truth. Had I broken into the house? I didn't think so, but I couldn't totally rule it out. My memory of the night started when the frat guys rushed in and confronted me on the couch. Why had I been there by myself? All I knew was that I'd been beaten up, badly.

Eventually, the cops came back to my window and asked where

I lived. I gave them the address on Eighteenth Street. Maybe they didn't want to do the paperwork, or maybe they didn't believe the frat guys who pretty clearly outnumbered and overpowered me. Whatever the case, they drove me home and let me go. If they saw me again that night, they said, they'd arrest me on the spot.

MAD

We were in Florida, visiting Pat at the University of Miami, when Alex called. Harry had been in a fight at a house near campus—his head kicked in, his eye socket badly bruised by the kick of a boot. When we called Harry, he described the battle in vivid detail.

What triggered the fight? Who knew. Something about a girl, Harry said. Some vanilla nonsense like that. No matter how hard I pressed, I knew I was not going to get to the truth; he would never give us a straight answer. My most immediate worry was the blow to Harry's head. I urged him to get to the hospital. He said no, but when we called him back to press the point, he relented. And Alex took him. The tests showed a fractured eye socket and a concussion.

Back at La Salle, I encouraged Harry to bring charges against the student who'd kicked his head in. An administrator was skeptical when I brought it up with her. She looked at me as though to say, "Mother, I know things that you don't know." I confronted her. What did she know about Harry? She was not at liberty to say—privacy and all. What crap. It made me dismayed and even madder than before.

Harry and I pushed the school to punish the student who'd kicked Harry in the face. As we waited in the hall for the official proceeding to begin, we saw the boy who attacked him surrounded by a whole team of people: student witnesses, parents, a lawyer, even a professor. There Harry and I sat, the two of us on our own.

At some point, someone from the school came up with a worried look on his face. "I'm sorry, Professor Dean, but Harry cannot have anyone else in the hearing. That's just how it goes, the rules and all, protection for the accused." The attacker, on the other hand, could bring anyone he wanted into the room.

The poor assistant to the assistant dean got an earful from me. "How about protection for the *victim*?" I asked. Harry deserved an advocate, just like the boy who attacked him.

"No, not at this stage. This is largely a student governing body review, with administrative oversight. Professor Dean, you can wait in the hall."

"Sorry, I'll be going in. I'm a professor here, a lawyer, and his mother. I'm going in."

We went in together, Harry and me. The room was long, stretching above the student union, with a wall of glass behind the "hearing body." The accused sat on the right, flanked by his team of maybe ten people, and Harry and I alone on the left.

The proceedings began. The accused claimed all sorts of criminal behavior regarding Harry, none of it previously revealed, and none of it connected to the night of the fight that left Harry with a fractured skull. There were accusations of vandalism, smashed windows, slashed tires, and Harry trespassing in students' houses. At one point in this litany, I had had enough. "If Harry is connected to so much wrongdoing that no one knew about," I said, "maybe he was there at nine-eleven, and we just didn't know!" It had gotten that absurd, and I wanted those around the table to know that we should be focused on the wrongdoing at hand: one student kicking in the head of another student.

In the end, the other student faced the consequences of his own wrongdoing. But as we left the school that day, I couldn't forget how coy the dean of students had been about her concerns over Harry. To this day, it baffles me. Under the guise of privacy, you know that a student is in grave trouble, even danger, and yet the university can say nothing to the student's parent—the person most likely to be in a position to help. Now there is an issue to work on.

And yet I wonder: Would I have listened? Could I have believed what I now wish she had said?

———

SIX

YOU CAN ALWAYS
COME TO US

HARRY

After the hearing, the school slapped me with academic and disciplinary probation. They had me on a short leash, but I wasn't deterred. I fell right back into my typical routine of smoking and drinking, snorting Percs, and passing out on the futon in Zach's house. Each day looked more like the last.

But when those two men held us up inside the home a few short weeks later, I found myself facing heavier consequences than a few pissed-off frat boys. This time, the assailants wouldn't answer to a college disciplinary board.

So I decided to drop out of school. I remember looking up my grades one day and seeing that I was failing every class. We were past the deadline for dropping classes, so my options were to be kicked out for my grades or show myself to the door. The assault, I realized, strangely gave me a chance to change the narrative. From the outside, maybe it would appear as if I was leaving on account of safety concerns, not my abysmal performance.

I dropped out and started working full time in the warehouse of my dad's bicycle business. For $10 an hour, I unloaded trucks, picked orders, and swept the floors of the cavernous space. The money wasn't great, but with no diploma and zero skills, it was the best I was going to find. Earning a paycheck sounded a lot better than sitting in school begging my parents for money. A small piece of independence.

I felt relieved to be out of school. The pressures of tests, assignments, and due dates were a thing of the past. Gone was my drive to succeed. My life was simplifying, shrinking.

MAD

All my adult life, I had known I wanted something more than teaching and practicing law. To be involved in politics—as a public servant, not a politician. There's a difference: A politician is someone whose arms draw inward, seeking to enrich himself and the people in his orbit. A public servant's arms reach out. Her work is all about others—doing things for people who cannot return the favor. Public servants prize and practice integrity, and they have the ability to spot their conflicts of interest and strictly avoid them. The difference is revealed in the pronouns they use: politicians pepper their words with "I"—public servants avoid the pronoun "I" and prefer "you" and "we."

I had seen the underside of politics when I worked as a committeeperson at age eighteen. One election cycle, an opposing candidate put out a mailing very close to Election Day that lied about our party's nominee. Cheating during our local elections? We were outraged, yet the mailer had come out just three or four days before the election—too close for our candidate to refute the lie.

We took action, forming a watchdog group within the local Democratic committee—the Fair Campaign Practices Committee, we named it. We met regularly, often at my house, to design fairer rules of campaigning, including restrictions on last-minute communications.

I loved thinking about ethics, and ethical practices interested me. And I loved the process of electing good people to office, playing even a small part in the public conversation. Someday, maybe I would take the chance to run and serve like the people we were working to elect.

The problem was when? And in what role?

HARRY

Shortly before dropping out, I had started dating a girl from La Salle. She stuck with me through the transition, a decision that strengthened my conviction. If I was such a failure, I thought, wouldn't she have left me by then? Having someone by my side gave me the feeling of self-worth that I couldn't muster on my own, though I knew she didn't have the whole story.

My girlfriend stayed in school to pursue her nursing degree, and I moved into an apartment in Bensalem, near the warehouse. I knew full well that I could never live with my parents again. My habit had grown to the point where it was all-consuming. If I went home, it wouldn't be long before I was failing drug tests again—this time for more than just pot.

If only I could go back to the partying of my past, I thought. To the simplicity and joy of those early nights on the golf course. But the withdrawal symptoms were now a constant weight that I carried with me. It used to be that I could save a pill, or even a half pill, for the morning—something to take the edge off until I could find more. But even that was becoming harder. I couldn't sleep until all the drugs were gone. Even then, it wasn't so much sleeping as passing out.

Maybe I could replace the pills with something less harsh, I thought. I became a home chemist, mixing alcohol, weed, Tylenol, even other prescriptions. But none of these mixtures were sufficient to replace my ultimate cure.

I made other attempts to curb my habit. I tried tapering myself down to a lower dose, but failed. I searched online for the least painful way of getting clean, but nothing worked. I took detox drugs, sometimes with limited success. Nothing lasted.

I had built my life in such a way that I was surrounded by dealers. Even in my loneliest moments, it wouldn't be long before my phone lit up with a text: "I'm good," meaning a dealer had just restocked, or "Thirties," meaning they had thirty-milligram Percocets for sale. My phone was like a pharmacy, and I had the prescription pad.

I was running out of options. In my darkest thoughts, I began to accept that I would die this way, that I wouldn't make it to my twenty-fifth birthday. But no matter how scared I got, I never thought about asking for help. That would show weakness. I had gotten myself into this, and I knew I had to get myself out.

Besides, even if I wanted to open up, who could I ask? My friends all used, and I knew my girlfriend would leave if she found out the extent of what I was doing. I couldn't even imagine asking my parents. While I knew my dad smoked pot back in the day, I had gone too far past that—what could they possibly offer? Not to mention the shame of having them see me for the junkie I truly was. Looking at my life, I saw just how alone I was.

MAD

By the time Harry dropped out of La Salle, I had been teaching English for more than seven years, and I was itching for a change of my own.

So I did three things: First, I asked Pat to help me find opportunities to run for office. Josh Shapiro was our community's young, talented state representative, I knew, but who was our state senator? If I didn't know, and most of my friends and neighbors didn't know either, maybe there was an opportunity to run. Second, I applied to a program at the University of Pennsylvania for people interested in government service. I would be the only fifty-year-old in a class of twentysomethings, but I needed the training. And third, I asked the chair of my department and the dean of the School of Arts and Sciences to let me teach part time, as I studied for what was next.

Both men said yes, while expressing that they were worried about me. Running for office is mean, brutal. Neither of them wanted to see me or my family personally attacked. This was 2010. In the political climate of those years, you were bound to see unjustified and downright false accusations, no matter what level of race you were running.

I had no idea what I was getting into, or just how bruising the race would get. But I assured them I was ready, that the chance to make a difference was worth the risk of ridicule. I was raised in a big family, the youngest of seven. Shots, jabs, and ridicule came with the turf.

The course at Penn had only just begun when I got the call. Michael Barbiero, the chair of the Abington Rockledge Democratic Committee, needed someone to run for township commissioner. "I heard you might be interested," he said.

This was still in the days of landlines. I remember wandering into our den with the wireless handset as Michael made his pitch. "No, thank you," I said after thinking for a moment. "I do want to run for office eventually. But when I do, it needs to be something bigger." Even then, I heard the naïveté in my reasoning. *It needs to be bigger.* Really?

Michael insisted that I run. This would be the perfect fit, he said. The current township commissioner, a hardworking and popular Democrat, had announced that he wouldn't seek reelection. Michael was determined and a bit desperate. When we said goodbye—after another polite "no" from me—I heard the disappointment in his silence. "Would you at least think about it?" he said at the end.

The call came at the beginning of a long weekend, when our family was traveling to ski in Vermont. We were hanging out in our rental that Saturday, January 8, 2011, when we learned that Congresswoman Gabby Giffords had been shot in Tucson along with eighteen others. I remember thinking: *What is wrong with this country? When will we see gun violence for what it is: madness?* More than thirty thousand people dying every year—some of them, like nine-year-old Christina Taylor Green, while going to meet their congresswoman at a local supermarket. Surely this would shake the marble halls of Congress. Would get our elected leaders to act. To legislate.

The events of that weekend brought some clarity for me. I knew I wanted to serve, so what was I waiting for? Maybe that call from Michael Barbiero had been a sign, had been the opening of a door.

That weekend, after talking with PJ and the boys, I decided to say yes. I called Michael back, and suddenly I was in the campaign. Michael explained that I should start by calling all the sitting commissioners and candidates to get their support. While PJ and the boys went out to ski that day, I picked up the phone and sat on the bed in our rented house looking out the window at the snow as I introduced myself to the commissioners from our area. I also called a few of my closest friends; most were interested and of course supportive. One was not. "Why would you do that?" she said. "Did you see what they just tried to do to a congresswoman?"

Ernie Peacock, the outgoing commissioner, was incredibly helpful as the race took shape. He came to our house and sat with me for hours, going over the issues facing the Board of Commissioners and showing me the nuts and bolts of running: knocking on doors, raising money to get my name and message out. The primary was in three months, and the general election in nine.

And so, while teaching part time and taking the class at Penn, I threw myself into the campaign for Abington Township commissioner, Ward 7. There I was, more than thirty years after my first local campaign, awkwardly going door to door on the streets of my neighborhood. On that first day, I went alone and empty-handed, with no pamphlet or calling card to leave behind. I did not do that twice. The next day, I printed business cards at home on perforated sheets. Later, I made a larger cardstock pamphlet and started walking with others. Whenever I missed someone at the door, I handwrote a message on my literature. "Sorry I missed you—Mad."

Some days, Ernie went with me, generously introducing me at the doors. My father-in-law, Bill Cunnane, sometimes knocked with me. He taught me a simple technique from his years of working as a door-to-door salesman of "brooms, brushes, mops, Ma'am": after you knock on someone's door, be sure to step back—giving the homeowner a safe distance from you, the stranger crowding their doorway. I still think of his advice with a smile each time I knock.

The campaign started in January and moved into the spring and summer of 2011. I knocked on thousands of doors that summer, trudging around in the heat with lots of help. By fall, I had gone around Ward 7 more than three times.

Door knocking is an interesting exercise. I will never forget the time my brother Bob and I were walking along a street and noticed a man working with a leaf blower in his front yard. We both hesitated, hoping he would turn the leaf blower down so I could introduce myself. Instead, he turned the leaf blower up, blowing debris all over us. Clearly not a vote that I was going to get.

Most folks either weren't home or didn't answer. But the ones who did talked passionately about local issues—traffic, development, taxes, and more traffic. Their issues informed my own. I set up a website and named it Abington 2020—a statement that our task in this election was to form a clear-eyed vision for our township's next decade.

I grew more confident with each pass through the ward. Not necessarily confident of winning—just confident that I was doing the right thing. Knocking on doors became a bit of a tonic. When something negative came up in my campaign, I would hit the pavement and talk to the people I was seeking to serve. The conversations had a way of taking my mind off the worries of the moment.

Including my worries about Harry.

HARRY

A year after dropping out of college, it looked like my luck was finally going to change. My girlfriend and I had been spending most of our time at my apartment after long days in the warehouse and at school. I was young and in many ways naive, but I always felt encouraged watching her pursue her degree. How she studied late into the night after going to class and hanging out with our families. We were in it together.

But in the last few weeks, we had noticed some of the usual warning signs of pregnancy. She had been tired—which wasn't unusual for someone splitting time between coursework and a job in the evening. But then came the nausea, irregular and abrupt. Morning sickness. We nervously made our way to CVS to buy a pregnancy test.

Back at the apartment, she took the test while I waited on the couch outside the bathroom. To my embarrassment, I found myself mumbling prayers of desperation. I hated the idea of God; I was an atheist, or so I thought. Yet here I was making a new plea for strength—a strength I knew I couldn't muster myself. "Please help me," I asked a God I didn't believe in, not knowing what to say. It had been so long since I had recited any prayer at all.

After a few painfully slow minutes, my girlfriend came out of the bathroom, and we sat on the couch waiting for the one or two lines that would determine our fate. But when the pink lines—plural—appeared on the display, my dread disappeared. Instead, a feeling of joy washed over me.

I was going to be a dad!

As we talked through our excitement and worries that night, I tried to comfort her. "We are going to figure this out, and you'll be an amazing mom," I told her confidently. I knew instantly the type of father I wanted to be. I was going to be just like my dad. Loving, caring, generous, and dependable. I also knew that drugs didn't fit into that picture. Maybe becoming a father would be my reason for finding a cure, a defining moment that would give me the willpower I'd desperately needed.

Then I realized there was an immediate obstacle to my happy future: telling my mom. She was a lifelong Catholic who believed in the sanctity of marriage. I doubted she would be thrilled that her twenty-year-old unmarried college dropout son was having a baby. So I decided to wait, looking for the best time to bring it up. *Maybe I'll tell her after I beat my habit,* I thought.

After hiding it for a few weeks and waiting for the right moment, I decided to call my brother Pat one night. He had graduated from college and moved to Washington, D.C., working in the Obama administration. We hadn't talked much since then, usually only in moments of crisis. But he knew my mom as well as anyone, and I needed advice. I remember standing outside my apartment, chain-smoking cigarettes as we talked on the phone.

When I told Pat the news, he demanded that I tell mom and dad immediately—not the advice that I was hoping for. It was late at night, approaching eleven, so I tried to buy myself time by promising to tell them tomorrow. Pat wasn't taking my excuses. "If you don't tell them now," he said, "I'm going to tell them for you."

I looked around the apartment complex. It was a beautiful early-summer night. The sky was dark and calm, but my heart had started to race.

I hated the idea of my parents finding out from Pat and not me. If I was going to be a father, I needed to show some responsibility.

"Okay, I'll do it," I said. I hung up the phone and prepared myself for another uncomfortable call to my mom.

As the phone rang, I breathed deeply.

MAD

Late one weekday evening, PJ and I were doing the usual: watching MSNBC and worrying over Harry. Would he ever go back to school? How could it be that he was working so many hours, yet not saving a dime?

Then Harry called.

As PJ talked with him, I muted the TV and listened to PJ's side of the conversation. "Harry, it's late," he said. "Mom and I are heading to bed soon. Can this wait?"

No, it could not. Harry was coming over.

"What's it going to be this time?" I said after PJ hung up. "Why the face-to-face meeting?" Already, my mind was cycling through the horrors of Harry's past.

But PJ was always kinder, calmer, never one to jump to conclusions. "Let's just wait and see what he has to say."

We spent twenty long minutes sitting in the darkened den, waiting. PJ in his usual spot, the corner of the couch, me on the edge of my seat, a small leather chair next to the couch. We wondered what bad news was on its way to us. Had he been injured? Was he in trouble with his landlord? Whatever it was, we knew it would be upsetting. Still, I did not see it coming.

"I've got some news," he said. "You're going to be grandparents. We're having a baby."

I slipped from the chair to the floor. *Oh, no, Harry, no.* I'd expected bad news, but not this.

In that moment, I cried. Cried for the boy whose blighted childhood had come to an abrupt end. Twenty years old and arrested in his development, somewhere a couple of years back. We had worried about our son navigating adulthood alone, let alone with a child. So I cried. Cried for the boy sitting in front of us, and the baby he would bring into the world.

There was so much to figure out. How far along was she? Pretty far: She was due in October, four months from now. I flashed back to a day a few weeks earlier when I had found her napping on the couch in our den. She looked so tired. The idea of pregnancy had flitted through my mind, but I'd dismissed it. Surely the two of them were smarter than that. I had always been in denial when it came to my boys and premarital sex.

"Has she been to the doctor?" we asked. Yes, Harry said, but only to confirm she was pregnant. They didn't have an obstetrician lined up yet. Did she even have insurance?

One of my first instincts was to implore Harry not to get married. An unplanned pregnancy should not be compounded with a hasty wedding. They were not ready for any of it.

I still remember how confident Harry looked when he walked into our house that night. A man on a mission, ready to tell us this big news. At one point in the night, he turned to PJ and said, "This will make me man up." He delivered that line with a salesman's smile, but for once, PJ's patience had cracked.

"No, it won't, Harry. What will change your life is when you get serious about what matters."

Manning up. PJ hated the expression. When one of his brothers screwed up, his father had always said the same thing. Some old Irish lie that men tell each other to make themselves feel better about their mistakes. PJ sharply corrected Harry: *This doesn't make you man up. You* determine your behavior, not an unexpected pregnancy. Just work, take responsibility, and that will reflect your wholeness. Manliness has nothing to do with it.

Over the next few days, there were dozens of phone calls, many with Pat. All of us worrying that these two were not ready. But we would pitch in. PJ and I suggested they live with us, to save money and have help taking care of the baby. To our surprise, they agreed.

A dark cloud settled over me, my worries about Harry piling up like his dirty laundry from years ago. We were all stumbling down the same imperfect path, but I took some comfort knowing at least we were on it together.

HARRY

After telling Mom and Dad the news, I turned all of my attention toward fatherhood. Step one: Stop using drugs. If I couldn't quit for me, surely I could do it for my future child.

Some of my friends had been arrested and sent to rehab centers. They told me about a drug called Suboxone, which doctors prescribed to help people get off of opiates. They said it helped with the cravings and withdrawals, that it made them feel "normal"—not exactly high, but not sick. They offered to let me buy their prescriptions from them. They weren't ready to stop using, so they had no need for a detox drug. The timing was perfect.

Suboxone came in two forms: a dissolving pill, or a sublingual film that dissolved under your tongue like an orange-flavored breath strip. The pills sold for less than the Perc 30s, only $10 each instead of $20. And because the drug was new to me, my tolerance was lower. Instead of taking five or ten a day, I only needed one or two.

Empowered by the Suboxone, I was able to quit Percs. I stopped smoking weed and doing coke. For the first time in years, it felt like I was clean. Like I no longer relied on getting high to cope with life.

Things were lining up for me to be the perfect father. I was ready to move back into my parents' house with my pregnant girlfriend. And if my mom ever pulled me into that bathroom under the stairs for a drug test, I took comfort in knowing none of the over-the-counter tests would recognize Suboxone. Finally, I would pass.

MAD

As we anticipated our first grandchild and worried over Harry's troubles, Larry got sick—terrible, flu-like symptoms. We rushed him to the emergency room, where a round of tests revealed tumors in his left lung and a buildup of fluid that would need to be drained regularly. Further tests confirmed the worst: stage four lung cancer.

The results weren't surprising for a lifelong smoker, but they shocked me still. My sister and our cousin Sarah and I feared the prognosis meant Larry would be gone in months. Yet, with the help of his doctors and his own quiet patience, he would live three and a half years more, enduring rounds of chemo and radiation, ports and procedures to drain his chest cavity. All without complaint. Even more impressive, he quit smoking along the way.

I'll never forget what happened one night a year or so into his battle. We were sitting in the dining room having a rare family dinner, and the kids started bickering. Whining about nonsense. PJ, looking to break the smallness of their complaints, turned to Larry and asked:

"So, Larry, how's the cancer going?"

Without missing a beat, Larry answered with a sly smile:

"Spreading nicely, thanks."

That shut the kids up, and we all laughed. That was quintessential Larry, finding the humor in the darkest of moments.

The summer brought changes as we planned for Harry and his girlfriend to move in with us. This was not an easy thing for me. Over the years, I had prided myself on perceiving—and meeting—other people's needs. My niece's need for a roof over her head. Walter and Larry's need for a family to support them through age and infirmity. Our house had become a place of welcome for many, but this new situation challenged me in a way that none of those others had. How could Harry have done this to himself? Did he really think he was ready to be a father?

One night, when I was a teenager, my dad initiated a surprising talk with me. I'd had no boyfriend and no prospect of even a date at that point—yet something possessed him to sit me down in our living room, with a charged sense of purpose in the air. "Mad," he said warmly, "you know that if you ever have a problem, if you ever find yourself in 'that' situation"—in other words, pregnant—"you can always come to us. You *should* always come to Mommy and me."

Now, forty years later, I thought back to that moment. It had left me speechless—the idea that my powerful father would display such kindness, empathy, and lack of judgment on an issue that I knew mattered to him. Why could I not offer the same to my son?

We set up three bedrooms and a bath: one for the baby, one for Harry, and one for his girlfriend. That's how hard I tried to control the situation: You are not married, not grown up, I reasoned, so you're not entitled to the accoutrements of marriage and a family. Still, I was proud of them—two young people facing the beginnings of parenting with a clear sense of commitment. But prideful enough that I wouldn't give up my firmly held beliefs that they should not sleep together under my roof. A naive thought, I know.

Early on with Harry's news, Pat saw how shaken I was. For days, I was just blue—lacking motivation when it came to the campaign. On top of that, the race brought me back to those first months of teaching at La Salle, when I walked into class feeling like an imposter: no Ph.D., no fancy credentials, nothing formal to offer these kids. I felt the same lack of confidence as a candidate. Did I belong? Could I win? Could I really make a difference, as I was promising the people who voted for me in the primary?

But Pat commanded me not to give up. A few days after Harry told us his news, he called from the White House. It always felt surreal, talking with Pat from the White House.

As I laid out my worries, Pat sharply counseled me: "Don't let this news derail you, Mom. Stay strong on your run for commissioner. Stay focused on that. This is your chance." Who was the parent in this situation? The fifty-two-year-old mother, or the twenty-three-year-old son demanding that she keep knocking on doors and win an election? How the tables had turned.

Harry was struggling with all sorts of problems—our family's mobile spinning out of orbit. But Pat wanted me to resist flying out of control with him.

Strangely, that was the same reaction I got from my godmother, Joan Cassin. Joan had been our next door neighbor and my mother's closest friend—a woman now eighty, with the spirit of fifty, who helped raise me and my siblings, and whose wisdom seemed to grow with age. One day, I stopped by her house to tell her about Harry—and to ask her advice. I remember sitting in her bright sunny living room and unloading my worries. I wanted her perspective.

As she listened, she got angry on my behalf. "No, Mad, this is your time," she said. "You and PJ have done everything for your boys. So do as I hope you will do. Deal with this, but remember that it is your time." An uncharacteristic flash of anger from Joan.

So we went to IKEA, and the soon-to-be parents picked out their furniture. As the summer went on, my heart softened, seeing the two of them preparing, making decisions together, building a small nest in our home. And after all, a baby was on her way!

HARRY

My new family's safety was of the utmost importance. Having lived through the home invasion and another unrelated stickup in a beer distributor that left me staring down the dark barrel of a handgun, I knew what had to be done. I needed to get my own weapons and learn how to use them.

Somehow I never blamed any of my misfortunes on the drug-fueled lifestyle I had been living. But that's exactly where the paranoia came from. After all, I knew all of the nasty shit I had done. Who's to say everyone else didn't have the same immoral tendencies?

When July 29—my twenty-first birthday—rolled around, I gathered my cash and ID and went to work, knowing I would have to wait until my shift was over to visit the gun shop. After researching for months, I had decided to buy a Glock 30 subcompact handgun. All day, I was unable to focus, obsessing over the Glock as if it were a new fix. A storm rolled through the area with powerful winds and rain. I sat at my cubicle, listening to the rain beat down on the roof as I quietly continued my research, watching YouTube videos and reading forums for gun owners. All to reinforce that my decision was the right one.

The second my shift ended, I jumped in my truck and made the drive to the gun shop. But as I pulled in to the parking lot, I was devastated to see a sign in the window: CLOSED. NO POWER = NO BACKGROUND CHECKS. After waiting twenty-one years, I hated to wait another day. But I had no other option.

The next evening, I made my way back to the gun shop and quickly passed the background check. After paying, I took a lesson on how to properly use and handle the gun. I had been watching videos on YouTube for months, so I felt like I knew the intricacies of the Glock 30 better than the instructor did. Still, believing that another violent situation was likely to happen sooner rather than later, I figured I should listen to anyone who might be able to help.

We weren't far removed from the shooting of Gabby Giffords, so gun control was a common topic of conversation at home. I had tried to sell Mom on the benefits of keeping a gun around for self-defense but had made little progress. We may have lived under the same roof, but we occupied far different worlds. My family's safety, however, wasn't up for debate. If we couldn't see eye to eye on guns, I would have to just keep mine hidden. Another secret from my mom.

MAD

For all his dysfunction, there's a quality that has always been innate to Harry, through thick and thin: Harry is caring.

During the pregnancy, the best of Harry came back into view. He took good care of his girlfriend all summer, making sure she was eating right, resting, and getting to the doctor. He seemed less focused on himself and his wild tales and more on the mother of his child. Even as his personal life continued to be a mess, his big, generous heart reemerged.

But the worries about Harry's behavior persisted—my antennae ever up. By now he was working full time with PJ, starting in the warehouse and then moving to the customer service team. But at home, I couldn't get over how he dressed. The stupid baggy pants that sagged below his waist, exposing whatever outrageous boxer briefs he was wearing that day. He shaved his head, shedding his gorgeous brown locks. And his fatigue became chronic. At times, he seemed too exhausted to participate in anything we did as a family. "I'm just too tired, Mom," he would say. "I gotta lie down. I'll do that right after I nap."

Meanwhile, I spent much of the summer going door to door in the hot weather, often with my father-in-law. The race seemed insignificant next to Harry's struggles, but I took Pat's advice and knocked on.

At one point, I asked my professor at Penn—Ed Rendell, the former Pennsylvania governor and beloved city mayor—to headline a fund-raiser for my run. If I learned one thing from his fantastic course, it was this: Ask. Don't be shy when it comes to stating what you need. If you don't ask, the answer surely is no. So into his Bellevue office I went, the middle-aged lady from the class, asking this political veteran to help with my small-time run for township commissioner.

The meeting was friendly, if brief. But when I came to the ask, the governor was stunned. "Mad—or is it Madeleine?—you are running for township supervisor, and you want me to head-line your fund-raiser? That would be unprecedented."

"Township *commissioner*," I corrected. "And yes, that's what I'm asking. Didn't you say we should always ask for help?"

That was it. I hooked him with his own teaching. I still don't know why he said yes. Years later, he told me that he thought I had only come to audit his course. Not me. I was there for real, for credit, I gave a damn.

We held the fund-raiser at our house one beautiful early fall evening. As the former governor made his way to the event that night, all I could picture was him saying to himself on the car ride there, "What the hell have I gotten myself into?"

We did not disappoint. The house was teeming with more than a hundred smiling Rendell fans, all of them incredulous that he'd taken the time to come to Abington for a township commissioner race. Rendell arrived and quickly asked for the "run of show"—the speaking agenda, I would later learn. We had planned for Rendell to speak last and close out the evening, but he told us he needed to go first. Something about heading to New York City for a cable show.

I must admit, PJ and I know how to entertain. Between the crowd, the food catered by a neighborhood restaurant, the music, and the generously staffed and stocked bar, the night was a huge success. And the reluctant governor gave the audience more than the price of admission. He talked for much longer than he promised and then took questions, clearly enjoying himself. When he left at the end of the night, he said, "What are you running for again?" We packed him a to-go platter for the ride to New York and thanked him for his generosity. We even gave him a special gift, a framed time line of some of his public service achievements.

I still remember the message of his talk: Elections matter, at every level. Who you vote for at the municipal level, at the state level, is even more important than who you vote for for Congress and president. It was a simple message, but fitting for the evening. Local elections affect you, every day of your life.

His audience beamed, and I beamed, too. This little girl from Glenside was a believer.

HARRY

Late in the evening on October 25, 2011, my girlfriend went into labor.

We had gone to the hospital the night before, under a false alarm. The doctors sent us back home to wait, but we knew we were close—that those nine long months were coming to an end. Now, in a bedroom in my parents' house, we timed the contractions with nervous excitement. And when the moment was right, we rushed back to the hospital.

I felt more than ready for my daughter to arrive. Our bags were packed, and the nursery was all set up. Most important, above all of the other preparations, I had managed to wean myself off the Suboxone.

That's right. For the first time in years, I wasn't addicted to any substance. I hadn't taken anything in two weeks.

With a clear mind, I watched the birth of my daughter, Aubrey, in the early hours of October 26. She was born a perfect, healthy, and beautiful baby girl. It felt miraculous. My plan was coming together flawlessly. A new father with his life back on track. I had everything I ever wanted, and then some.

"Thank you, God!" I whispered when the excitement died down.

With that false sense of confidence and excitement, I texted Mark a picture of my daughter along with a short message. "Baby girl is here and healthy, you've got to come meet her and celebrate with us!" The next morning, my phone lit up with his reply, "Congrats, Bro! I'll be there tonight." I couldn't wait.

That night, he showed up with a nice card—and a bag of celebratory Perc 30s. For some reason, as I walked down to the parking garage to find Mark's car, my fear of falling back into the grips of addiction was nowhere to be found. My short stint of sobriety had brought me a false sense of total control: If I could stop once, I could certainly do it again. That's why I didn't think twice before snorting Percs with Mark in his car. The negative memories of using were utterly obscured. I could see only the positives—how the effects of those blue pills would add to the high of the moment, my joy at the birth of my daughter.

As Mark and I sat in his car, smoking cigarettes and snorting the fine blue lines, I bragged about my success in quitting.

"It's easy," I told him with a dollar bill rolled up between my fingers. "All you have to do is taper yourself down with Suboxone. The withdrawal wasn't even bad. Let me know if you want to try it, I'll walk you through it."

"I'm so happy for you, bro," he said with genuine sincerity.

I was blind to what had just happened. I couldn't see the sadness of relapsing in the parking lot as my newborn child lay in the hospital. All I saw was the momentary bliss that I knew would come from snorting a line of Percocet into a clean system.

We went back inside to spend some time with the baby, then I walked Mark back out to his car. "Can I have a few more?" I asked, believing that this was just a onetime celebration. Tomorrow, I would stop again.

The problem was, tomorrow didn't come. Within twenty-four hours, the withdrawal symptoms were back, and I found myself sneaking out of the hospital to find a dealer. I picked up right where I had left off.

When we brought my daughter home from the hospital, I realized that I was stuck. The body aches and cold sweats had returned with a vengeance. So had the overwhelming obsession to find more. "If I just use this one time," I justified, "I won't be sick, and I'll be able to stay up a little later with the baby. I'll have the energy to go back to work after a sleepless night."

I found a new source of Suboxone and switched over to that. I even distanced myself from my friends and dealers like Mark—which was easier to do now. Whenever friends tried to meet up, I would tell them I had to stay in with the baby. "Soon," I'd promise.

In truth, I felt ashamed. I had just bragged to them about getting my life on track for my daughter. But a couple of months went by, and I was still taking Subs. And now I was taking more than ever. My habit was up to eight or ten pills a day.

Night after night, I would hold my daughter in the rocking chair in the corner of her nursery, staring at her beautiful face as she slept. She was perfect, adorable, with a patch of brown hair and big innocent hazel eyes, just like me. I could see her entire life ahead, filled with possibilities, potential. The same opportunities I had once squandered to drugs.

"Please help me," I whispered to her through tears. "Help me to be better for you, to be the father you deserve. I know you deserve so much more, and I'm trying, I need you to know I'm trying." The desperation turning to anger, to defeat. "You don't deserve this," I said.

I begged my daughter for the strength to stop using. But I couldn't do it. In those moments, I was caught between the sickness of withdrawal and the relief that the Subs brought. I'd convince myself over and over again that if I used one more time, I could take better care of her. That if I wasn't sick, I could read her the bedtime story, or rock her to sleep. But the desperation gave way to darker thoughts. Who's to say that my daughter wouldn't be better off without me? I was an addict. Broken, hopeless, and completely out of ideas on how to change.

MAD

On the day of the election, Aubrey was just eleven days old. I remember feeling thrilled to share this day with my new grand-daughter.

Our strategy was for me to spend the day visiting and working the three polling places in Ward 7. I started at the Abington Free Library, the polling station where I would cast my own vote. There is a strange ritual that takes place at the polls. Depending upon the location and the players—committee people and campaign volunteers—the Democrats line up on one side, Republicans on the other, with signs, placards, and literature in hand. As soon as they see an approaching voter, the workers rush over to hand out a sample ballot and plug their party's candidate.

Like the weather on Election Day, committee people can go from bright and sunny to cold, competitive, rainy, and rude as they vie for votes. Sometimes the tactics get nasty: removing signs and literature for the opposing party, or improperly marking sample ballots. Even pulling people aside to tell them some lie about the opposing candidate.

As I worked the library that day, I texted Harry, reminding him to come and vote. Forty minutes later, he arrived with Aubrey in her infant carseat. I sat with her in the vestibule as he marked his ballot—proudly showing her off. Susan, one of our neighbors, glommed on to us like Mrs. Kravitz from *Bewitched*.

"Susan," I said, "have you met our beautiful new granddaughter, Aubrey, born October twenty-sixth—just eleven days ago?"

Susan looked sidelong at our beautiful baby. "Oh, I did not know any of your boys was married," she mock-asked.

"None of them is, Susan."

Susan looked back with an air of disgust. "Oh, I'm sorry," she said.

"I'm not," I said, turning my gaze back to Aubrey.

When the polls closed that evening, I stayed behind at the

library with a watcher's certificate that allowed me to observe the count. Back at home, people were getting ready for a party. We had invited the entire local Democratic committee to our house as they awaited the final count for all of the elections, up and down the ballot.

Before long, the township commissioner's race was called. I had won in a landslide.

HARRY

A few months after my daughter's birth, I got a call from Mark's brother. "Mark's in jail," he said. I wasn't surprised. Mark had gotten DUIs before. "What is it this time?" I asked.

"Manslaughter," he said after a long pause.

My heart dropped as he told me that a close friend had died after using drugs with Mark. It was a combination of Percs and Xanax—the same regimen I had consumed to excess time and time again. *It could have been me,* I thought. I could have been the one going to prison. Or the morgue.

I went online and searched the news. Immediately, Mark's face appeared. A mug shot for the whole world to see. I was crushed. Mark had never wished harm on anyone. He was just like me. But somewhere in his long chain of desperate acts, his luck had run out.

I thought about how many times I had put myself in the girl's position, using drugs indiscriminately while assuring myself that it would never kill me. Then I realized: Until the very end, she must have thought the same.

MAD

In January 2012, I was sworn in as an Abington Township commissioner. At the ceremony, I wore a corsage, placed my hand on a Bible, and promised that I would uphold the Pennsylvania Constitution, so help me God.

A rabbi I did not know, Larry Sernovitz, offered a special prayer during the ceremony. A prayer full of wishes to guide our service.

"May God bless you all with discomfort at easy answers, half-truths, and superficial relationships, so that you may live deep within your heart," he said. "May God bless you with anger at injustice, oppression, and exploitation of people, so that you may work for justice, freedom, and peace. May God bless you with tears to shed for those who suffer pain, rejection, starvation, and war, so that you may reach out your hand to comfort them and turn their pain into joy. And may God bless you with enough foolishness to believe that you can make a difference in the world, in our Commonwealth, so that you can do what others claim cannot be done."

I liked the surprising nature of the prayer, especially the hope that we would be foolish enough to believe that we could make a difference. That was exactly how I felt.

In advance of the night, I'd been given the agenda for that evening's first Board of Commissioners meeting, which would take place immediately following the pomp of the swearing-in. We got right to business, but as the session went on, the idealism of the rabbi's prayer gave way to a sense that something wasn't right.

On the agenda for debate was an ordinance that would require putting government contracts above a certain amount of money out for public bid. I voted in support, and so did the rest of the committee. Good governance. Yet, jarringly, later in the night, we were called upon to reappoint our township's solicitor for a new contract. The decision was sailing through when I awkwardly interrupted the vote. "Wait a minute," I said. "What's the total value of the contract for legal services?" It was well over the threshold we had just set for a public bid. "Have we sought other bids?"

The sitting solicitor and the board president rolled their eyes, clearly annoyed. "Pay no attention to her," they seemed to say,

"Mad is clearly new and doesn't know how things work." I tried pointing out that we had just passed an ordinance that required competitive public bids for contracts of high value, and the solicitor's legal bill topped $100,000 each year. Why would we not require the same scrutiny for legal services? In a split second, the merriment of the evening faded. The solicitor of many years, offended by my questions, tried to explain his billing and hourly rate. And the board took the vote to renew the solicitor's contract. I voted no, and lost.

I had made everyone uncomfortable—including me—yet I knew I was more comfortable in the discomfort of asking than sitting quietly by in the unease of acquiescing. That would be my role on the Board of Commissioners: questioning the status quo, questioning the way things were done.

Within weeks, I would face a difficult decision of my own. Josh Shapiro, our sitting state representative, had run for county commissioner that fall. His was a historic run, a chance for Democrats to take the majority of the three-member Montgomery County board for the first time in more than a century. Josh won big, becoming the chair of the County Board of Commissioners. There was only one hitch: He would need to resign from the Pennsylvania State House.

A year earlier, I had told Michael Barbiero that I wanted to run for something bigger, a chance to serve on a greater scale. This was it. In short order, I would need to decide if I wanted to run in the special election that would soon be called by the Pennsylvania Speaker of the House.

While I was determined, I fretted over the decision. It was so soon after my run for township commissioner that I worried the optics weren't good. Would I be seen as too "ambitious"? Somewhere along the way, that word had become derogatory— especially when directed at a woman in politics. The more I thought about it, the sillier that worry seemed. I decided to take the next step.

A run for state representative would be different from a local race. First, I had to interview with an eleven-member search team, who recommended a handful of candidates to the local Democratic Party. Then you campaign by calling all seventy-plus members of the body and making your case. I came to that first interview armed with a written plan, mimicking the one I'd written for my class at Penn. It was a crowded little room in Josh Shapiro's old campaign office, almost not big enough for the twelve of us to sit in a circle. They went around the room asking me questions. I did my best to answer, speaking confidently about the things that I knew, and believed—honestly about those I did not.

On the night of the nominating vote, we were down to three candidates. The search team supported me, and it was agreed that the other two candidates would accept the committee's recommendation. Things looked all set—until one of the other candidates reversed course midmeeting and placed her name in nomination.

We three candidates gave our speeches. Mine centered on a theme that was coming into focus for me: the Three E's that would guide my campaign if I became the nominee: education, the economy, and ethics. I was nervous as I made my case, but I could tell that the room was receptive. A vote commenced immediately after the speeches. I won, with the third candidate calling for a unanimous vote by acclamation.

It was settled. I would be the nominee. Off and running again for a special election not yet scheduled by the Speaker of the Pennsylvania House.

HARRY

At one point, my friends with Suboxone prescriptions were cut off by their doctors, so I started going to back to Kensington to buy the Subs. As I drove into the city that first day, the whole arrangement felt wrong. This landscape that once excited me was now in such stark contrast to the life I wanted. Driving past the familiar streets—Somerset, Allegheny—was a grave reminder of just how far I had fallen.

Since my daughter's birth, I had tried to change my look. The baggy jeans and T-shirts gave way to khakis and button-down dress shirts. If I couldn't stop using, at least I could look like I was doing better.

But my new look didn't fit in on the Ave. As I drove toward Kensington, I would change in the car, slipping on a dirty sweatsuit that was covered in burn holes from dropped cigarettes and tucking my pistol into my waistband. I needed to fit in everywhere I went, and this felt like the best uniform for copping drugs. It made me less of a target to be robbed, and I wouldn't stick out as much to the passing cops.

I would park my car around the corner and walk down the Ave with purpose. Passing the homeless people and addicts who lined the street, I envied their lives as I perceived them—lives with no family, no responsibilities, no expectations. What would it feel like to be freed from responsibility, from the fear of disappointing my family? Could I finally let go of the emptiness that I felt? Would I feel peace?

But I never got the chance to find out. After buying the drugs, I would rush back to work or home, where my girlfriend and daughter waited. I went back to a life where I was failing miserably. With each lie, each secret trip to the city, I hated myself more.

MAD

I felt a clarity, a sense of urgency, about the run for state representative. This was my chance to make a difference.

We set up shop in a single-story space next to the Abington police station and the offices where I'd been working as a commissioner. Josh Shapiro had used the office for his campaign.

Either he had left in the night without packing up, or he'd generously decided to leave us most of the infrastructure for a campaign office. In any case, we were grateful to have it.

We got to work. And by we, I mean, *they:* the staff and volunteers. As a commissioner, I had represented five to six thousand people in a single ward in Abington. If I won this seat in the Pennsylvania House, I would be representing more than sixty thousand. I had no idea how to run a campaign at this level, except for the power of knocking on doors.

Thankfully, we were surrounded by a diverse group of friends, family, and political veterans who wanted to see us succeed. PJ and I invited them into our living room, these dozens of party players and influential people, and asked their advice: What would the run involve? How much would it cost? What did they think about my making so quick a move after having just been sworn in as commissioner? I was unknown to many in the Abington and Upper Dublin Democratic communities, and I wanted everybody to know that I wasn't taking this run lightly.

There is a wonderful randomness to the people whose orbits you cross in politics. There was PJ, of course. We met more than forty years ago—as kids, really, now with kids and grandkids of our own. How lucky was that? More recently, there was Kathleen Joyce, the manager of my campaign. I remember the day I met Kathleen in 2008 during Barack Obama's first run. Like millions of others, I was inspired by the candidate and was looking to volunteer. I wandered into a bright, strangely painted makeshift headquarters. Seated at a desk was Kathleen, directing the traffic of volunteers, barely looking up as I asked for materials. I remember thinking, this gal is in command—if a bit intimidating. That began our connection. No more than five foot three, with a voice like Kathleen Turner's and long strawberry red hair, Kathleen had the mind of an accountant and thought in spreadsheets. There was a spreadsheet for everything—from budgets, to the ground game, to Christmas cards.

For the state rep race, our homely yet homey office hummed with activity. Kathleen headed a great staff. There was Mark Koenig, a policy expert who had worked for Josh Shapiro; David Floyd, who kept his eye on the dollars; Michael Barbiero; Neil Deegan, an experienced congressional fund-raiser; and eventually dozens of volunteers. One of the volunteers, Koh Chiba, worked with my niece Caroline at a local restaurant while majoring in political science. He started out taking video and pictures for us, but quickly proved he had a talent for campaigns, then a talent for constituent services, then a talent for policy. Eight years later, he's my chief of staff in Washington, D.C.

On that first campaign, Kathleen and Mark took point on our overall strategy and the groundwork necessary in the field—canvassing, Election Day poll coverage, and the gathering of volunteers. I remember sitting in that little room and dialing for dollars for the first time. Neil drilled me in the art of "call-time": dialing for dollars and contributions. That part was painful. We started with my "Christmas card list," close friends and family, before moving on to other well-known Democratic contributors. We made cold calls, trying to make a connection with complete strangers before awkwardly asking them to contribute. Most of the time, we had to settle for leaving voicemails.

Around the time I got the party endorsement, a Republican entered the race. This was a special election, so we did not know how much time we would have before the election was called. I threw myself fully into the run, dismissing the worries that it was all too much: teaching part time, taking another class at Penn, working as a township commissioner, and on top of it all, managing my worries and battles with Harry.

Finally, the Speaker of the Pennsylvania House weighed in: The special election to replace Josh Shapiro would take place on Primary Day, April 24, 2012. Which meant I was now, in effect, running for the special election to complete Shapiro's unexpired term while also setting myself up for an additional run. The seat would go up for election again in the regular cycle in November of that year.

There were nights when my head would not allow me to sleep—racing with worries over whether I was smart enough to do this, whether I was nimble enough, tough enough. True to my friends' expectations, the run did come with some blows and some cheap shots. In the worst of them, one of my opponents conducted a cheesy telephone poll including the question "How would you feel about voting for Madeleine Dean if you knew she had been disbarred?" I had not been disbarred, and he knew it. When a friend told me about that call, it made me sick to my stomach.

My team took quick action: We called an election lawyer, sent a cease and desist letter that day, and demanded to know how widely the poll had been circulated. I was relieved, witnessing the help that surrounded me, but still felt sick and distracted. Guess what the cure for that ailment was? Door-knocking, the tonic. I slowed down, walked the streets of our community, and listened as my neighbors told me about their own worries and hopes. Just as with the run for township commissioner, it worked.

We ran an aggressive, professional campaign, hiring a firm in D.C. to design our mailers. I felt proud of two mailers in particular: one from our campaign, and the other from my opponent. The first was a beautiful, tri-folded piece with a photo of me standing in a sea of spring pansies at Penny's Flowers, Glenside, where I worked my first job through junior high, high school, and college. The idea was to introduce me and my roots.

I would have paid money for the other mailer, but I didn't need to, because it was sent by my opponent. It was a picture of President Barack Obama next to a classically grainy picture of me, with the caption "Madeleine Dean & Barack Obama, extreme liberals, perfect together." I was so proud to be mentioned in the same sentence with President Obama that I beamed when I first saw the mailer. We framed it, and it now hangs in our bar at home.

On election night, we once again held a party at our home, inviting the entire local elected Democratic committee and the countless people who had supported our run. Kathleen, ever the numbers guru, needed a quiet space where she could collect the results after polls closed at eight o'clock. We stationed her in the basement, the bunker, away from the gathering crowd upstairs, with a monitor that displayed the incoming votes. But people kept slipping downstairs, surrounding her, trying to snatch an update. Soon so many people packed the basement that I worried there might be no one left upstairs.

As the numbers rolled in, and Larry continued to bring down trays of hot pigs in a blanket, the mood in Kathleen's bunker grew more and more exuberant. "What do you think?" I said. "Do I have this?" No one was offering me that assurance, not yet. Then, finally, with 64.2 percent of the vote, Kathleen and the others confirmed: I had won.

Now that was a party! Our house burst with the enthusiasm of friends, family, and colleagues who had spent all day working the polls, everyone feeling thrilled that their work had paid off.

HARRY

Maybe I wasn't yet as resigned to that horrible fate as I thought. I had one more idea, one last plan to stop myself from using drugs. I decided to become a police officer.

Mom had met some local officers during her campaign, and the job seemed interesting. If I became a cop, I reasoned, I would have to stop using. So I started taking the necessary steps. I bought a book to study for the police exam. I took practice tests online. I even met with a local sergeant for breakfast at a diner. He told me how he'd gotten into law enforcement, and said it was a tough but rewarding career. As we ate, I asked questions about the academy and the hiring process. I told him that I wanted to make a career change, and he encouraged me.

I left breakfast reenergized. Some local departments were hiring, and I knew I could ace the test.

MAD

May 6, 2012, was a head-spinning day. As I entered my small office in the Pennsylvania capitol—twelve by fifteen feet, with a dark wooden desk, a couple of chairs for visitors, and a sofa—there was a banner welcoming me with my title and picture. I thought of my mother's sweet smile. My, how she would have loved this.

The Pennsylvania legislature is the oldest in the country, dating back to 1682. The capitol building, as it stands today in Harrisburg, was dedicated on a gloomy fall day in 1906, when President Theodore Roosevelt rolled into the city by train and called the structure "the handsomest building I ever saw." As I stood for the swearing-in ceremony, I was in a state of near disbelief over having the privilege to serve in this historic House. Of the six members being sworn in that day, I was the only woman.

I remember putting my hand on the Bible, the gravity of that moment weighing on me. How I wanted to hold on to that feeling, the weight of my oath of office, for as long as I served. I thought again of my parents, and of Wally, hoping they would guide me and give me the strength to serve well.

After the swearing-in, the House took a break before transitioning into session. As people filed in and out of the chamber, a large African American man in uniform walked up and warmly congratulated me. He was the chief page, responsible for answering any member who pushed the call light at their desk, whether they needed help printing vote records, connecting us to guests, or collecting our floor remarks for entry in the record. As he guided me up the side aisle to my seat at desk 84, he shook my hand and said, "My name is Wally. I'll look out for you." And I believed him.

Wally would look out for me. How I needed to hear that.

HARRY

On the morning of the test, I drove to the local high school, placed a strip of Suboxone under my tongue, and walked in with a couple #2 pencils in hand. The applicants had gathered in the cafeteria, with a few officers who had come to administer the test. I watched as they paced the room, noticing the guns they were carrying— .40 caliber Glocks. I envisioned myself going through the rigors of the academy. Surely I would have the most accurate shots.

The test had multiple parts, asking how you would handle different ethical and legal situations. Then there were questions testing your general academic competency. It was all in line with the books I had been studying. No surprises.

I walked out of the cafeteria confident, finishing the test well before the time expired. I hadn't been in school for a while, but I still had it.

A couple weeks later, the results came back. I had aced the test. The police department wanted me to take the next step—a physical assessment, which I knew would include a drug test. I tried yet again to taper down from the Subs, but with no success. All of the strategies I had used in the past weren't working. With a baby at home, I couldn't subject myself to the withdrawal. I needed to be present, I couldn't be sick. I had to be there for my daughter. I was using against my own will, but I had to accept it. The catch-22 of being a parent and hooked on drugs. When the day came for the physical exam, I knew there was no way I could show up.

That morning, I made my way into the kitchen and saw my mom. I quickly reached for my back, and pretended to wince in pain. "I really hurt my back. I don't think I can perform the physical exercises today."

She didn't reply.

"I'll reschedule soon," I added, trying to sell the lie. "I'm so mad I can't go today!"

She nodded subtly, showing her disappointment and her clear lack of belief. Still, the lies flowed without hesitation. All I had was the hope that she would buy my excuse as I sank back into the hopelessness I knew so well.

MAD

Around that time, I was beginning to learn about the increased illegal drug trade crisscrossing Pennsylvania and our country. In open budget hearings, we would hear directly from the state attorney general. She described how the scope of the problem was growing, becoming more violent and deadly, especially with the introduction of Fentanyl. I learned of the trade in illegal heroin, smuggled in from Mexico, China, and other ports of entry. It was a cheaper alternative to prescription opioids, and many Pennsylvanians were taking it.

I did not allow myself to connect Harry to that epidemic. As much as I believed—knew from those home tests—that he was involved in drugs, I never allowed myself to think it could be cocaine, or worse. I believed Harry was using, just not an "addict." I don't know what I was thinking. I guess I pictured him going to foolish pill parties with his college friends—as if I had any idea what that meant.

My eyes were opening to the epidemic consuming our community. Yet I remained blind to the idea that the very scourge ravaging the Commonwealth I served could be the source of the sickness in my own home.

SEVEN

A GATHERING STORM

HARRY

When you're using, each day feels like a hurricane. Every call, every conversation, could be the one where you are confronted with the truth—not the truth as you see it, but the truth as it is seen from the outside. The fear of getting caught consumes you. You can't stop chasing, you can't stop lying, and you can't stop using. To stop is to risk being exposed. So you continue to spin.

As desperation took over, it became easier to cross new items off my list of nevers. For one, I started stealing. In the past, there were times when I took cash and drugs from dealers or friends who I thought wouldn't notice. They were the kind of guys who would steal your wallet and help you look for it; I knew because I was one of them. It was easy to justify that these people deserved to be robbed. But that line soon became blurred. I reasoned that stealing for my daughter's formula and diapers was okay—even noble—ignoring that my entire paycheck had gone toward drugs. With this new thought, everyone became fair game. And now the targets in my crosshairs were the people who loved me the most.

The first time I stole from my dad's wallet, I sat in my room for hours, debating whether to do it. My dad had a mantra: "What's mine is yours." He said it all the time to me and my brothers, but I knew this was not what he meant. He left his wallet in the same place each night—on the kitchen counter near the back door—and I knew his ATM code from the times when he asked me to get cash for him. It seemed too easy. I promised myself that I would replace the money as soon as my next paycheck came. As long as I followed through, it would be more like borrowing, not stealing.

I started with $100. An easily repayable sum. But before long, I was going back again night after night, upping the ante. It became $200 per trip, then $300, with the money adding up faster than I could repay it. I hadn't been caught, but I lived on pins and needles. My mom kept a close eye on the accounts and the bills. Every time we crossed paths in the kitchen or she called while I was at work, I froze and waited for the accusation.

I thought back to my high school days, when I'd tried drugs for the first time. I was a kid, hardly through puberty, but making decisions that would change my entire life. A sense of dread settled over me. I didn't know whether it would be overdose, suicide, or prison; all I knew was that life wasn't sustainable the way I was living it.

I thought of my mom, newly elected to political office. Her opponents had been grasping for straws, trying to portray her as extreme. I could see their next mailer in my mind. "Madeleine Dean can't even manage her own home. Imagine what will happen to our district on her watch." She loved her work. I couldn't bear the idea that I might take it away from her.

I thought of my girlfriend. What would happen to her if I got arrested, or worse? And I thought of my daughter, only a few days away from her first birthday. She was the only person on earth I had opened up to about my struggles. How could I do this to her? How could I deprive her of her relationship with her father?

In the middle of all this, the news was consumed with a different storm than the one happening in my life. Hurricane Sandy was bearing down on the mid-Atlantic.

As a drug addict, you learn to hate anything outside the norm. Anything that makes buying drugs more challenging. Holidays become a burden (even drug dealers want to spend Christmas with their families), and snowstorms make it risky to drive to your dealer. This weekend's approaching hurricane was no different. Philadelphia's mayor, Michael Nutter, was preemptively closing major highways and warning that there could be power outages across the area. The National Weather Service said massive winds and flooding were imminent. One thing was clear. I would need to stock up enough drugs to last me through the weekend.

So I did what had become my routine over the last few weeks. On Wednesday night, I sat in the basement listening for my parents' footsteps in the kitchen above. Before bed, they would always make a pass through to turn out the lights and lock the back door. This was my signal. As they brushed their teeth, I would tuck my Glock 30 into the holster on my waistband, the gun's black handle making a slight bulge under my shirt. When enough time passed, I snuck outside and made my way to the ATM in the local convenience store at the bottom of the hill. In the cold October air, it was easy to wear a hoodie without looking out of place.

On my way into the store, I was careful to look down and avoid eye contact with the cameras. I approached the ATM from the side and placed my palm over the camera as I entered the PIN. A familiar anxiety washed over me as I punched in the amount—a physical reminder of how wrong this was. Three hundred this time. (It would be a long weekend, after all.) As I counted out the twenty-dollar bills, I felt a slight semblance of control, knowing that the money would give me to ability to re-up on Suboxone. I could control my sickness, manage my withdrawals, and be present for my daughter throughout her birthday weekend.

MAD

Harry peeked his head into our bedroom late one night. "Mom, could I borrow a little money? Just till payday?"

My anxiety was up again. I had just hung up from talking with PJ, who was traveling for work. We talked about the usual: Who had he met with? What city was he headed to next? Then we moved on to the worries at home. Aubrey's first birthday was coming, and no one seemed to have a plan. Then there was the problem with our bank account. Before hanging up, PJ told me he had reluctantly given Harry a little money earlier in the week—and would I please pay the American Express bill? We had enough money, I said, but my last trip to the ATM revealed a balance way too low. What should have been five or six thousand was only five or six hundred. Now Harry was asking for more.

I told Harry I couldn't give him anything. There was something wrong with our account, and I had to straighten it out in the morning.

That was it: An unpaid American Express bill unlocked the madness.

As I walked into the bank the next morning, I had no idea what was what. We were in the final two weeks of the campaign, a blur of speeches, debates, meetings, train stations, and door knocking. I sat at the banker's desk and overexplained that I was running for reelection to the Pennsylvania State House— guessing she would neither know nor care. I hadn't been checking my bank account, I said, but surely there should have been more money in it.

The banker pulled up our account and asked if we were in the habit of using the ATM a lot. Like, every day or every other day. She turned her screen so I could see a recent history of the last three weeks: Night after night, a series of ATM withdrawals had drained our account. Two hundred dollars this night, $100 the next, $300 another—$4,300 in total, gone.

"I think someone is stealing from you," she said. "Do you want me to call the police?"

Confused for a moment, I asked her to print out the statement. Could she identify whose card was being used and where?

It was PJ's card, she said. Used locally, often at Wawa, and always late, around midnight.

A few crazy thoughts bolted through my mind. Had I somehow lost all that money? Had PJ spent it? But then I knew. "No, thank you," I whispered to the banker, and muttered something about a family member. Out I went to the car to sift through the evidence of the theft—the draining of our account night after night.

And I pictured Harry, going down to the kitchen after we had gone to bed, to remove PJ's card from his wallet and sneak to Wawa for cash. Then back home, to the counter by the back door, to slip the card back into place. What a lonely, depressing scene.

I sat in the car and called PJ. "I know it's drugs," I said when he picked up. "Harry is stealing money from us. That's why I can't pay American Express."

The weekend was crazy, as our house often was. PJ came home from his trip to find me in full campaign mode, and the two new parents stewing over Aubrey's first birthday. How to celebrate? What should she wear? And a too-expensive cake. I was mad at both of them. A one-year-old does not care about the cake or clothes. Why didn't they dress her in one of the beautiful unworn dresses in Aubrey's closet? Why not bake a cake at home? No, that was not their vision.

As I look back now, I realize that we were also in the throes of Superstorm Sandy. I have almost no memory of the hurricane, though—I was focused on the storm inside our house.

Over the course of the weekend, I gathered bank statements and lined some things up. For the first time I could remember, PJ and I were seeing Harry's situation through the same lens. There were no "I told you so's" from me, and PJ no longer needed convincing. The bank statements were clear. We talked for hours about our fears, about our plan for confronting Harry. Would we need an interventionist? And what was the best course of treatment? In the past, both of us had been through attempted interventions with family members who were struggling. But it felt different now that it was our son.

There is something uniquely desperate about a son stealing from parents who are willing to give him everything.

Eventually, we came up with a plan. We would get through the weekend, with the storm outside and our granddaughter's first birthday. After that, PJ and I would confront Harry with the bank statements and the truth.

And then—God willing—he would agree to go for help.

HARRY

I had seen this coming since Friday.

Just before the weekend, my mom mentioned a problem with her bank account—the balance wasn't right. That one little offhand comment sent chills of fear through me. I knew if she looked closely into her account, she'd find it. A litany of ATM withdraws made in the middle of the night. As hard as I'd worked to cover my tracks, the only thing I couldn't account for was the missing money.

The strange thing was that my mom hadn't pressured me at all over the weekend. The house seemed calm, which was unusual for us. Sunday's party came and went without a blowup, and Monday passed without incident. But on Tuesday, my mom called me into the family dining room. It sounded innocuous enough, but I knew it wasn't. We never used that room, and it was still morning. Something wasn't right.

Our dining room is the most formal room in the house, with an elegant mahogany table that my parents purchased from the previous owners. When we moved in ten years earlier, I remember noticing that this furniture was nicer than anything we had ever owned. There is a button on the floor beneath the table, hidden under the thick, regal carpet. If you pressed it, a buzzer would go off in the kitchen. A way to call for help.

Now I was sitting in that dining room with my parents across from me—the two people who loved and supported me more than anyone else—and my girlfriend at my side. Bank statements were splayed across the too-nice table, with transactions highlighted. I didn't have to examine the documents to know what they were. I could see the disappointment on my parents' faces, mixed with fear.

"Harry, you are stealing from us, from Daddy and me," my mom began, in light of my silence. My eyes watered.

"You need to tell us what is going on," my dad added.

I was silent. My gaze fixed on the documents, avoiding eye contact. I couldn't bring myself to speak.

After my mom's comment on Friday, I had spent days trying to come up with a believable excuse. I'd always been able to spin a story—it was the skill that had gotten me out of everything else until this point. But this time, as I reached for the words, there was nothing. Just the truth. I had stolen from my family. My drug problem was completely out of control.

I remember my mom crying as she told me what she'd discovered. I remember not being able to get a word out, only tears. But the fear of exposure was accompanied by a new feeling: For the first time, the truth seemed safer than telling another lie. This was my moment of clarity. Suddenly I could see that my parents were just as afraid as I was. That maybe, just maybe, I hadn't been alone in my struggles. Maybe I had been dragging them through it, too.

MAD

"Harry, you remember how I told you there was something wrong with our account? Well, I figured out what it is . . ."

I don't remember saying much more. "You're stealing from us. From daddy and me. It's got to be for drugs." Harry's face looked broken, his big eyes darkened and filling with tears. For the first time in years, it seemed he had nothing to say.

He admitted that it was drugs. Suboxone, he said. I didn't know what to believe, but I knew instinctively what to ask. It was the only question that mattered to me and to PJ.

"Are you ready to get help?"

And his response: "Yes."

I couldn't believe it. Harry said yes.

How was that possible? I had been told, schooled, counseled that we would need an intervention, and an interventionist. When I asked Harry if he was ready for help—and he said yes—I cannot describe the happiness, the joy I felt.

Don't get me wrong. I was scared to death. But I was so hopeful. I saw in his teary eyes that he was telling the truth—in a single word, "yes," rather than some grand, fanciful story. I connected with Harry again. The dense curtain of lies was falling.

And so, in the craziness of our house—amid the stacks of campaign materials and the remnants of a one-year-old's birthday party—the four of us went up to the master bedroom to call the Caron Foundation, a treatment center in Pennsylvania. I put the phone on speaker as Harry, his girlfriend, PJ, and I found places on the floor and the bed. The intake specialist introduced herself and asked some questions, her voice almost singsong, as though she were selling a timeshare. But I quickly dismissed those judgments. All I knew was that we had to get started, and we had to go today.

Harry was twenty-two, so they would place him in a young men's program. The counselor advised us on things we should pack—what was necessary, what was allowed. Could he smoke? That was a big concern. He could not. He would be allowed cigarettes only for the first day or two as they processed him through the detox wing.

After the call, we reviewed the packing list and divided to conquer the chores. Someone would need to run out for toiletries. I did not want it to be Harry, fearing that he might not come home. But Harry insisted—he and his girlfriend needed the time alone together to say goodbye. As we scurried to gather things he would need, I called my two top campaign colleagues and asked them to come over. The election was a week away—they needed to know.

Kathleen and Mark sat with me in the living room.

"There's something you need to know," I said. "You know I've been worried about Harry and have been battling with him—and there's something we've discovered. He's been stealing from us to support a drug habit. Thank God, he's agreed to go for help. He's going today."

A flash of fear went through me. What if my opponent figured this out in the last week of the campaign and dragged our family through the mud?

Neither Mark nor Kathleen thought first of the campaign. They told me not to worry, that they had it under control. "Focus on this," they said. "The campaign will be fine."

HARRY

As I packed that day, the reality of leaving for a month began to set in. What had I agreed to? Could I really leave my daughter, her mother, my family, and my job for thirty days? What would people think? Surely they would notice I was gone.

In hindsight, there is never a perfect time to go to rehab. But in that moment, the fear was overwhelming. Would my daughter be okay? Would my relationship with her mother last? The hypotheticals were endless, and the more I played them out in my imagination, the more afraid I became. Questions like these had kept me from asking for help for a long time. But now it wasn't up to me. I had to go.

It was almost time to leave. My girlfriend and I decided that she would stay home with Aubrey while my parents drove me to the treatment center. There was only one thing left to do. Get rid of my drugs.

I snuck into the garage, where I had hidden my last Suboxone, and placed the strip under my tongue. The moment of clarity in the dining room was still fresh, sitting at the front of my mind. But I had been so conditioned by my addiction, I was unable to throw away a high. I told myself that I deserved this last measure of peace.

Even then, I noticed a change. Normally this was when I would panic and start plotting to find the means to get more drugs. But not this time. This time, as I stood by the garage looking at the downed trees in our neighbors' yards, strangely not in ours, all was calm. It was a turning point in my life, though I had no idea how significant. I felt a brief moment of calm—and not just from the drugs dissolving in my bloodstream. There was peace in my mind, and a slowing of my racing thoughts.

The truth had come out without killing me. I wasn't disowned or even yelled at. I had been so obsessed with covering my tracks, it had kept me from seeing that all my parents wanted to do was help me.

MAD

There were reasons I was set on Caron. Our family had a long history with the place.

In the 1970s, my uncle Wally ran a Catholic retreat house in a handsome stone manor on the hill across from the original treatment center. For five or six Thanksgivings when I was a teenager, my big immediate family would join our cousins,

Uncle Walter, our grandparents, aunts, and uncles, for a rowdy, fun weekend. Upon arrival, Wally would greet each of us at the base of the long, winding driveway and hand us a postcard of the place that showed our room assignments.

Years later, Walter left that religious assignment for whatever he was asked to do next, but he always stayed friends with the family who owned the treatment center across the way. Eventually being asked to say the funeral masses for both Dick and Catherine Caron. And, sometime in the 1980s, our dear friend Larry went to Caron, or Chit Chat as it was known (not happily), for treatment for alcohol use—becoming an extraordinary example to all our boys of humility and self-deprecating strength through humor. Larry was a caretaker to the core. He had a servant's heart, always thinking first of others, whether it was his dearest friend Walter or our kids. That's the kind of guy Larry was. His true self could have been obscured forever if not for his time at Caron.

So it was Caron. Nowhere else. Wally's spirit was there.

After three long hours of packing, PJ and I got into the car with Harry riding alone in the back. The hourlong drive was quiet. I lost count of how many downed trees we saw along the way. Yet even in the aftermath of Superstorm Sandy, the day could not have shone brighter to me.

At one point in the drive, I broke the silence. "Harry, did you ever think of asking us for help?"

"I did," he quietly explained. "But it just never seemed like a good time. You know, with Larry sick. Then there was Christmas, Easter, Mother's Day, birthdays, the elections, Thanksgiving . . ."

After a long pause, he added, "Maybe, there's no such thing as a good time."

There are two expressions about addiction and recovery that I hate: *He has to hit bottom,* and *He has to want to get help.* What the hell is the bottom? Where is it? And how are we on the outside supposed to recognize the exact moment when our loved one is ready to accept help? But that other famous expression—the one Harry offered in the car—rings true to me. There really is no good time to ask for help.

On my way out the door, I grabbed a bland, blank notecard, knowing I would not be able to communicate with Harry for a while. As the car lapsed back into silence, each of us running through our own private worries, I scribbled something on the notecard. I wanted Harry to know how I felt. To know that although this was what people called "hitting rock bottom," it didn't feel that way to me.

As we drove to Caron, I tried to get my bearings from the decades before. The manor house on the hill, standing like a lighthouse drawing us in. But that's not where we were headed. We parked and checked in to a lower-level set of offices, lit anesthetically.

In the quiet hallway, PJ and I waited for a minute or two as Harry underwent a brief intake process. I was filled with hope—yet half sick with fear. What would detox be like? How sick would he get? How lonely? I hated that I wouldn't be there to help him. And there was the question hanging above it all: Would Harry stay? I worried that he would renege on accepting—or at least fully buying into—help. My head raced with worry over how we would handle things back home, with a mother and a baby coping with their loss and my election just a week away.

The intake folks called PJ and me back to go over some of the final details: When would we be able to hear from Harry? How would he be treated during withdrawal? How did family visits work? Then, before we knew it, it was time to go. As we left, I hugged Harry and said, "I love you, and I'm proud of you." And I was.

As PJ and I walked outside, I felt scared, and I'm sure Harry did too. But much more than that, I knew we had a chance. The lying was over; the unseen fires in the walls of our house were out. And as I thought about the initials tattooed between Harry's shoulder blades—WRD—I knew my son would not be alone.

Wally had his back.

HARRY

I feared what the note would say. What could she possibly be writing?

The car ride took only an hour, but it felt like a silent eternity. I couldn't help thinking about everything that had brought me to this point. Sure, I had made a few bad decisions. But somewhere along the way, I had crossed a line. I went from swearing I would never even drink alcohol as a kid to using drugs against my own will. Getting my skull broken, having guns pulled on me in a home invasion, and watching friends get sentenced to years in prison hadn't been enough to stop me. The wreckage of the storm was pervasive.

I didn't know what to expect from rehab. I knew it was where drug addicts went, but I had no understanding of what took place there. Some of my friends had gone because their parents sent them, or their lawyers thought it would help reduce their sentence. None of them had managed to stop using after they got out.

Still, I had always thought the lucky ones were those who got to go. The son of a politician and a successful businessman didn't belong in rehab. I couldn't do that to my parents. And if I'm being honest: While I knew I had a drug problem, I never considered myself an addict. To me, an addict looked like the characters from *Requiem for a Dream*. I didn't fit the image of a homeless junkie in filthy clothing, and I never shot heroin. Hell, by this point, I was only using Suboxone, a drug meant to wean people off the ones that really mattered.

I compared myself to every drug user I knew, searching for

anything that would distance myself from the others or tell me I didn't belong. Since then, I've learned that the disease of addiction doesn't discriminate. In the coming months, I had a lot left to learn.

When we arrived at Caron, it was getting late, nearly dinnertime. In a blur, the staff took me through the intake process—a series of interviews, searches, and a quick physical exam—all while talking with my parents separately. When my parents finished their part of the process, a staff member interrupted my interview so I could say goodbye.

In the lobby, the three of us hugged quickly and said "I love you." There wasn't much time for anything more than that. But as we pulled out of the hug, my mom looked me in the eyes and said something that I was not expecting: "I'm very proud of you, Harry." It caught me off guard. How could she be proud? Under the circumstances, it seemed like she should only feel anger, disappointment.

She handed me the card she had written in the car, and I walked back from the waiting room into the treatment center. In the back, I was searched by a large, gruff man who carefully removed everything from my bags and placed it on a table. He opened the shampoo bottles, examined every pocket, and checked to make sure I had nothing on me. When I asked why he would search someone who was voluntarily going to treatment for help, he smirked slightly. He didn't have to say anything. Until this moment, I had snuck drugs with me everywhere I went. Just showing up at rehab didn't prove anything.

After the search, I met with an intake specialist who asked me questions about my drug use. I wasn't sure if I could be completely honest. How much of this would get back to my parents? I guess that's why they took urine samples at the end of the interview. A staff member then escorted me to the room where I would spend the night. It was located in a small detox wing, with a few comfortable hotel-style rooms and a "lounge" that looked like the waiting room in a doctor's office. Outside, there was a small white gazebo where I could go when I needed a cigarette.

I don't remember what I did that night or when I went to bed. I only remember waking up at five to a nurse taking my blood pressure. Already the withdrawal symptoms were kicking in. My whole body ached, and I couldn't get back to sleep. The racing, worrisome thoughts returned. What were my parents doing right now? How was my daughter taking this? Could I really live like this for thirty days?

I stumbled out of my bedroom, dripping with sweat and hunched over in pain. In the lobby, a nurse sat behind the counter. She appeared to be around my age, only she had cat whiskers drawn onto her cheeks. "Happy Halloween!" she said cheerfully, but I was in no mood for small talk. I asked her for one of the cigarettes from my stash and made my way outside.

I sat down in the gazebo and opened the card that my mom had written to me in the car. It was a simple card with flowers on the front. I was afraid of what it might say . . .

30 Oct 2012

5:15pm

My Dear Harry—

It seems so strange to be driving to Caron on the heels of the terrible storm Sandy—but the day seems bright to me. This ~~should be~~ is a very good day for you: you have asked for help—the help you need to be healthy, happy, well. I love you. I'm proud of you. As worried as Daddy and I have been, I have such optimism and confidence in you. You are an amazing young man of many gifts. You are smart, handsome, kind, loving, funny. Addiction has tried to bury your gifts. Don't let that happen. Reclaim them all for yourself and that will be the greatest thing you could ever do for your adoring Aubrey. I love you more than you know! Daddy too.

Mommy

Remember to pray often—to God, to Walter, to my parents. Nothing is impossible with the Lord.
XXOO
Written in the car—Sorry so sloppy!

I took another drag of my cigarette and stared at the card, searching for the optimism my broken mother had expressed. I didn't feel it. I wasn't ready. I was still mourning the loss of my life, the only life I had known.

A tear slowly made its way down my cheek, but I didn't wipe it, just let it fall.

EIGHT

THE LIFE
IN HIS VOICE

MAD

As we drove down from the mountaintop where Caron sits and on toward the highway, my mind raced back to how we had gotten here. "What did you think when Harry said there was 'no good time' to ask for help?" I asked PJ.

"I don't know . . . I was surprised, sad."

"I always wanted the boys to know they could come to us—to me—with anything. It scares me that he would've hidden so much."

I had a primitive understanding of addiction, informed by my father's work at SmithKline and as a writer and editor of the *Psychiatric Reporter*. As early as the 1970s, he talked about addiction as the product of disease, not moral failure. From a young age, I knew addicts were not bad people. At least in theory.

I was relieved to have Harry in the program at Caron—in any program. We were on a new path. Yet I was scared. I knew withdrawal would make him sick, but I knew I didn't comprehend how hard it would be. The specialists had tried to ease our worries. They explained Harry would be watched very closely and offered comfort medications when appropriate. Still, the stories we heard at intake were harrowing. There were patients who simply left treatment in the night, desperate for more drugs. Eloping too often to death. I couldn't shake the thought.

Please, God, I thought. *Please, Mommy and Daddy. Please, Wally—keep him. Keep Harry there.*

HARRY

I couldn't stop thinking of the note my mom gave me. Her pride, her optimism. I wondered how she could write such positive words at a time like this. I had lost all faith in myself, and the nice yet sterile setting of the detox unit did little to inspire confidence.

As I looked around the rooms in the treatment center, the walls were lined with 12-step posters that said JUST FOR TODAY or THINK, THINK, THINK. Others left it to a single word like COURAGE or SERENITY. All of them so clearly aimed at inspiring us patients, as if their optimism could flow right off the walls and soak into the broken people who walked past.

What had I gotten myself into? Going to treatment had seemed to be my only option as I sat at the dining room table, confronted by my parents and the proof of what I'd done. It had seemed like the easy way out—and I was used to taking the easy way out. But now, as I watched the other patients, some of them elated, others shattered, everyone recovering in their own way, it reminded me of the work I had to do. "It only works if you work it," I heard over and over. I hated work, and although everyone in the unit had been broken in their own way, I wondered if it was possible for me to be fixed. After everything I had tried, what did I have left to give to this process? What if I gave this all of the fight left in me, and it didn't work?

MAD

After dropping Harry off, I went back to campaigning. The election was only a few days away. As I braced myself for the rush of that final week, I thought about how different my life looked than it did a few years before, when I was a mom watching her kids start grade school, or a professor daydreaming about maybe, someday, getting involved in politics.

That week, there was plenty of turmoil in our house: most importantly, over the baby, and how we would all pitch in to try to smooth the path for Aubrey and her mom. From the moment we set out for Caron, PJ went into MacGyver mode, maneuvering cars and altering work schedules to ensure that mother and baby were cared for, physically and financially. I knew in my gut that treatment was the only way for Harry to be a father at all. It was about saving his life—so he could parent, be a daddy to Aubrey. I don't know if the rest of the family saw it that way, but as for me, I always had a grave sense that this was a matter of life and death.

In a strange way, saying goodbye to Harry reminded me of when we dropped off Pat at college. There is a moment as a parent when you know you don't belong, you cannot do this big thing for your child. You must leave, look back, and say, "Goodbye, I have confidence in you. I'm proud of you. I love you. You must do this with your own effort. I just hope you don't feel alone."

That's how it was with Harry. Only this time, I knew there was much more than a college education at stake.

HARRY

The first couple days in detox were a blur as I shuffled between four different locations: a twin bed in a double room with no roommate; the white gazebo, where I sat smoking and contemplating how the hell I was going to get through the next month; passing time in the rec room; and visiting the nurses' station for frequent checkups. The nurses would ask how I was feeling, check my blood pressure, and test for contagious diseases like TB. Most important to me, this was where they administered my "comfort meds," to help taper me down gradually from opiates. We also took diarrhea and nausea medication to help fight the awful symptoms of withdrawal.

The rec room was a modest space with green walls and a window that overlooked the sprawling campus and the mountain that loomed above it. The room had comfortable couches and chairs forming a U shape around a small TV stocked with sappy PG-rated movies on DVDs and VHS tapes. I spent lots of time in there talking with the other patients.

One was an older man in his fifties or sixties—though decades of alcoholism had aged him well beyond his actual years. As we talked about how we had wound up in the facility, he told me that this wasn't his first experience of going through rehab. This time, his kids had dropped him off. I thought of my daughter and the possibilities for her life: either having a father who was present, or having to drive me back to rehab someday. She had just turned one year old. I couldn't fathom surviving until she was old enough to drive, let alone stomach the idea of using for that much longer.

At the end of the conversation, the man told me something important. "I wish I were in your shoes," he said. "To get ahold of this so young, with your entire life ahead of you."

I stared at him blankly, not knowing whether to be encouraged or scared. After all, he had been to rehab before and it hadn't worked. Would it work for me? What might my life look like if it did? Or worse, if it didn't?

There was a priest at Caron, a staple on campus. He was an Oblate father, like my uncle Wally had been. On Sundays, he held a chapel service that was open to all the patients in the facility. Standing at the altar, he appeared authoritative, with a full head of white hair. But his broad smile invited you in, and his blue eyes were free of judgment. Growing up, I had hated going to church, the archaic formality of it all. Chapel with Father Bill was different. It felt engaging and honest, grounded in a spiritual, yet not religious way.

When I passed Father Bill in the cafeteria one day, he asked how I was doing. He listened as I complained about the life I thought I had destroyed. Then he said something that stuck with me: "You are not a bad person trying to be good, Harry. You are a sick person trying to get well." I had always thought the opposite, that my actions left no doubt that I was a bad person. For once, I allowed myself to consider that I might not be the piece of shit that I had always thought I was. I thought of the tattoo of Wally's initials on my back. Sad that I had thrown away countless opportunities to get to know him better, but comforted feeling his presence. Even if I wasn't ready to buy in, I knew Wally would have said the same about me.

My job at Caron was to begin understanding addiction as a disease. This was a new concept to me, and I wasn't sure that I really bought it. I knew that I was an addict and that I needed help to get clean. But I had always hoped there would be a day in the future, after I'd gotten enough distance from the withdrawal symptoms, when I might be able to have an occasional drink, like a normal person.

But the first week of treatment shattered that notion. Early on, one of the counselors held a group session to teach us how addiction worked. After asking us to share our experiences with using, he showed us in depth how any mood- or mind-altering substance could trigger our addiction, snapping us right back to the depths we had so recently begun climbing out of. All it took was one taste, and the obsession and compulsive behaviors would consume us again. As he talked, I thought back to the night at the hospital when I snorted the pills for the first time after a couple of weeks of abstinence. There was no easing back in. Staying clean was an all-or-nothing affair.

There were other assumptions I had to unlearn. Assumptions

that had once protected me, and insulated my problem. I originally thought that if I went away from my family, I wouldn't have to live with the disappointment of having failed them in so many ways. But as the reality of life in rehab sank in, I realized that my old world would go on without me in ways that would make it harder to return. When I left this place and went back to my life, what would people think? Would they see me as the junkie who robbed his family blind and abandoned his girlfriend and daughter? The one who couldn't put the drugs away, even for them? I spent much of the first few days alone in my room, cycling through those questions.

One day, in the middle of these thoughts, a nurse interrupted me and told me to pack my things. It was time to leave detox for the primary unit at the top of the hill. The medical staff had stabilized my withdrawal with a dose of Subutex and would begin weaning me off over the next few days. I had nothing to pack, so I asked if I could smoke one last cigarette before leaving. She handed me two Newports and buzzed me out the door.

Outside at the gazebo, I savored each inhale, the only familiar comfort I could pull from this situation. With each drag, I tried to prepare myself for whatever was waiting at the primary building. The concept of not being able to smoke really pissed me off. I was a junkie, for God's sake. What was a cigarette going to do? "These people really just don't get it," I muttered as I walked back inside. A nurse led me to a van, and I rode uphill to the building for young adult men.

Once inside, a counselor's assistant named John gave me a quick tour, leading me down a cinderblock hallway, past a recreation room and a group room with beautiful floor-to-ceiling windows. Then he dropped me off with my counselor for a quick introduction and a run-through of the rules and expectations. The counselor told me what time to wake up (early), when to go to sleep, when to eat, and where to show up for "groups," the 12-step meetings we were required to attend.

"Welcome," he said. "You can go to your room and get settled."

As I walked out of his office, I couldn't help thinking about my daughter. I was supposed to be raising her, teaching her how to live. Yet here I was, my life reduced to a confined space with a regimented schedule and a clinical staff telling *me* how to live.

Then, right there in the hallway, a familiar voice bellowed behind me with a laugh: "Are you fucking kidding me?"

I turned around and saw him. It was Dave, one of my closest friends from high school. Dave had been at Mark's brother's place on the night when I first tried cocaine. Now here we were, reunited in rehab. He walked toward me with a huge smile and his arms open for a hug.

Dave gave me the lay of the land. "It's not that bad," he said. "Almost everyone is cool. You just have to watch out—some of the counselors are harder than others, and they are trying to send everyone to aftercare. But you've got a kid, so you don't have to worry about that."

I nodded, taking it all in as Dave showed me to our next group. It was a patient-led 12-step meeting. I had no idea what to expect, having never been to one of these before, but I had years of practice fitting in—at least superficially. Whether I was in the presence of drug dealers, my family, or visiting my brother at the White House, I became a chameleon, acting the way I thought others would want me to.

As the group meeting started, everyone went around the room introducing themselves. "I'm Sam, and I'm an addict." "I'm Dave, and I'm an addict." And on and on.

By the time my turn came, I knew exactly what to say. "Hi, I'm Harry, and I'm an addict." The words rolled off my tongue without hesitation. Maybe I was just trying to fit in, or maybe I had known it deep down for a long time.

I have no memory of what anyone else said. But as I listened to the other guys, I realized for the first time in my life that I had found a group of people open to speaking their truth. They, too, had lived life as chameleons. And the stories they shared freely were some of the very secrets I'd planned to take to my grave.

MAD

We couldn't talk to Harry for many days, maybe a week. And the first phone call was challenging. He was youthfully combative: "This is not going to work. This place is ridiculous. There's no cigarettes, just some lousy games and super-PG movies. They even withhold the coffee if someone acts up."

"Who acts up?" I said.

"This week, John jumped on a bed and broke it. Kyle is trying to sneak cigarettes. And we *all* get punished for it."

It sounded like we were back in junior high. And in many ways, we were—with Harry surrounded by twenty or so housemates in a young men's dorm, all of them struggling to reclaim their adulthood from the ravages of addiction.

"I gotta see Aubrey," he said at one point in the call. The distance had been tough for him and his girlfriend, he explained. "I could do this at home."

"That's ridiculous, Harry. You know this is the best place for you."

The details were different, but here we were, fighting again. And it was only week one.

HARRY

For the first week of my stay, I was placed on a blackout. No calls or texts—no contact whatsoever with the outside world. Just me and the other patients from the program. We all had left varying degrees of wreckage smoldering back home, and the time to address it was not now. We were here to focus on our recovery, learn how to survive, and stop the slow suicide that each of us had been engaged in.

I wavered between loving and hating the blackout. Hating it be-cause I still had the self-righteous desire to do damage control with my girlfriend; loving it because it helped me avoid the mess I had made of my life.

When the blackout ended, a counselor handed me a stack of mail. I was surprised to see that my aunt Maryann had written me a letter nearly every day. Maryann is my mom's sister and the mother of my three closest cousins. She wrote almost all of her letters on a yellow legal pad, usually with some sort of quote attached. In one, she included the front page of *The New York Times* from October 31, with images of the devastation Hurricane Sandy had left behind. AFTER THE DEVASTATION, A DAUNTING RECOVERY, the headline read. It seemed apt. Another time, she sent me a list of famous musi-cians, comedians, and actors. "Do you know what all of these peo-ple have in common?" she wrote. Then the answer: "They all struggled with addiction, and they all became their best after they stopped drinking and using drugs." Every letter had the same sign-off: "We're rooting for you, Harry."

I deeply appreciated the letters. They gave me a break from the monotony of life in the facility. Still, each time I read them, I lacked the courage to respond. My mom's sister was being open and hon-est with me. Was I ready to be so honest with the world?

I had the same struggle once I regained phone privileges. My calls with my mom and dad were hard. They asked how I was doing, how I felt. And I could generally only reply with something like "Good" or "Okay." I told them about the food and the antics of the other patients. Surface-level stuff—nothing deep or revealing. When we spoke, I felt like a child.

I thought about how much money they'd spent sending me to this place. Saying it wasn't cheap would be an understatement, and I could only imagine the anger my parents felt. Yet they had sup-ported me freely and without hesitation, willing to invest in my fu-ture, and in my life. They knew my past, and they were willing to try again.

MAD

As PJ and I searched for the right treatment center for Harry, we learned the price. I knew treatment was expensive and presumed our health insurance wouldn't cover much. But I had no idea just how expensive it would end up being.

I was ignorant of so many things. Ignorant, yet determined Harry would go to Caron regardless of cost. I know I was lucky to be able to say that. And PJ did not fight me. He did have his assistant look into alternatives, less expensive places that might have done a good enough job. We considered them together—me, only dismissively.

But how were we to pay for it? I went through a mental exercise: Sure, Caron was expensive, but so was Pat's college tuition and Alex's, and so would Harry's have been if he had stayed in Charleston. On the ledger of our kids' lives, I reasoned that the first one had gotten college tuition and the next would get treatment for addiction.

It was a way to justify the expense on Harry's behalf, but I quickly felt ashamed for keeping that mental ledger. Who compares lifesaving medical treatment to college tuition? Maybe a mother who is determined, yet ignorant.

HARRY

So much was happening for others. My mom was running for a full term as state representative. My brother Pat was traveling the country with President Obama, as he campaigned in the lead-up to the 2012 election. My brother Alex was off at college, and my girlfriend was living with my parents and caring for our daughter alone. Me, I was stuck.

On November 6, America went to the polls—but for me it was just another day in rehab. I went to groups, to the cafeteria, and back to more groups. At night, we gathered in the rec room to watch the election results. I was eager to see how it turned out. Had my mom won? Had President Obama?

I wouldn't find out that night. We had a strict bedtime, and the counselor's assistants (CAs) weren't going to break our routine for something like that. As I watched the footage of President Obama on the news, I thought back to the previous spring, when Pat got our family into the Easter egg roll on the White House lawn. On the way in, a Secret Service agent had me place my cigarette pack in a bin to be searched. I panicked. There were tabs of Suboxone clearly visible, hidden only beneath the clear cellophane. But the panic turned to thrill when they handed it back without noticing. I felt ashamed, recalling that moment. But that's who I was. I needed to have drugs with me everywhere I went.

I thought of Pat flying on Air Force One and wondered where I could have been had I followed in his footsteps. And as I went to bed dreading another sleepless night filled with aches, pains, sweat, and restless legs, I wished I could have been with my family on such an important day.

The next morning, my mom sounded excited when she picked up the phone. "We won!" she exclaimed. As I sat in my counselor's office listening to her describe Election Day, Aubrey, voting with her, and the victory party, I tried to force excitement into my own voice.

"That's great! I knew you would," I said. "Sorry I couldn't be there to vote for you."

MAD

Early on, our calls with Harry were monitored by the staff at Caron. Harry would sit in an office with a counselor as PJ and I joined the call from different locations, listening for signs of hope amid Harry's small talk and criticisms of the facility. But the call at the end of his second week went differently.

At first, Harry went through the usual complaints:

"I've got to smoke. I need to be home with Aubrey. I don't need to stay here. I've got this."

Then there were new concerns.

"How long is this going to take? I heard twenty-eight or thirty days, and now I'm hearing they're probably gonna tell me to stay longer. *Aftercare?* It's gonna cost a ridiculous amount of money, Mom, and I'm not doing it!"

As our volley went back and forth, I owned up to the fact that I knew twenty-eight days were never going to do it. Treatment was a much longer haul. During the intake process, the staff made clear that withdrawal alone could take a couple of weeks. And I had begun reading and researching what it takes to recover from opioid addiction. Most poignantly, I learned from other mothers—specifically my friend Lucille, whose son had been to Caron—about the long road ahead. To have any hope at recovery, you needed to rewire the patient's brain, and that can take months when you're dealing with young men. The odds were already stacked against us. We needed as much time as we could get.

But beneath Harry's complaints, something else was different on that call. His voice. As we talked, I beamed to myself. Ever since his slide into active addiction, his voice had morphed into a low monotone. But now, there were tones and sounds and inflections that we hadn't heard in years. Harry's lighter, livelier voice was back.

After saying goodbye, PJ and I hung up and immediately called each other.

"Did you hear that, PJ? Did you?"

"Yes, Mad, I did!"

We were both crying, reveling in the sound of our son's voice. Our son was back. And we heard hope for his recovery, all sung out in the sound of his sweet voice.

NINE

WAR STORIES

MAD

Thanksgiving is my favorite holiday, the one day a year when my cooking shines. Sometimes I cook two turkeys, just to be sure we have loads of leftovers. Christmas, by contrast, is too much pressure: I'm a lousy shopper and get worked up trying to find presents for everyone.

When I was a kid at 208 Roberts Avenue, the house would teem with food, kids, grandparents, great-aunts and -uncles, cats, and a dog wagging her tail at all the fun. Our family's traditions have changed over the years, with the cast of characters growing in some ways, and shrinking, sadly, in others.

Thanksgiving 2012 was a strange mix. We certainly had a lot to be thankful for: Harry in treatment, and a beautiful granddaughter in a high chair next to the table. Pat growing in his work for the Obama administration while Alex settled into college and PJ grew a company. And me, officially elected to my first full term as a Pennsylvania state representative. I loved the work—the chance to learn more and to speak up about things that mattered.

There was so much love. And yet so much worry, much of it unspoken. Would Harry make it through recovery? What would it take? How long? All told in an empty chair around an otherwise bustling Thanksgiving table.

HARRY

As I looked around at the other patients, I judged who I thought would relapse and who might stay clean. Some guys had been in and out multiple times and didn't seem to want it at all. But there was another group of us who seemed to sincerely want to change.

Sam was one of the patients in the second group. He was a smaller blond-haired guy around my age. He didn't speak often, but when he did, his quiet voice offered real encouragement and sincerity. Sam talked openly about his struggle to get along with his parents, and he pinpointed exactly what he was feeling. As I listened, I hoped I could have that level of honesty one day. All I knew was whether I felt good or bad. And without drugs, it was almost only bad.

It was hard to stand out as a troublemaker among this crowd, but some of the guys managed. They were loud and always causing problems with the CAs. I pictured myself falling somewhere in the middle, happy to trade war stories with the troublemakers or exaggerate how serious I was about recovery to the CAs. I was still acting like a chameleon.

When Thanksgiving rolled around, the symptoms of withdrawal washed away any festiveness I would have felt. I hadn't slept in days, and my body ached. The counselors held gratitude meetings throughout the day in which patients were supposed to share what they were grateful for. "My family," one guy said. "Not using drugs today," said another. "To be alive." These were the common themes.

I had no grasp on any of that. I felt miserable missing Thanksgiving with my daughter, my family.

When I called home that night, my mom answered. She was in the dining room with my entire family. The table, once covered with those telltale bank statements, was now loaded with the traditional fixings of a Thanksgiving dinner. Mom passed the phone around, and I spoke to everyone briefly. I couldn't help being embarrassed. No one made me feel that way; they were all so positive, so proud of me for seeking treatment. But as I sat there looking around my counselor's office, the walls were a strong reminder of the reason I wasn't there with them.

MAD

When we dropped Pat off at college, we went through a series of orientation meetings. Parents sitting in a circle in a large meeting room, with a box of tissues in the center, to discuss biggies like homesickness and roommate conflict. Even to a mother dropping off a son at college for the first time, the whole thing felt a little dramatic. A sappy indulgence for parents and kids of privilege.

Family weekend at Caron was different. A sobering three or four days of meetings, seminars, and exercises meant to help us understand our children's condition and the ways in which we as families could support their recovery. I can't remember whether the staff gave us tissues. If they did, we would have needed more than a single box.

The long weekend was our chance—our obligation—as a family to join Harry in treatment. Pat and Alex joined, too, for one of the days. We shuffled between sessions on a range of topics: the progression of substance use from treatment through early recovery; the danger of relapse; how to create effective boundaries; the myths and truths of enabling addiction versus supporting a loved one in recovery. I was mighty proud of Pat and Alex, who participated willingly, even if they looked a bit bug-eyed, as if thinking, "How the hell did we get here?" They were behind Harry four hundred percent, with no questions or resentment. Just the love that only brothers can express.

Between them and the other family members supporting from home, PJ and I felt so lucky seeing the love that surrounded Harry, each of us trying to get the mobile of our family back into balance, trying to understand the roles we each played.

When the counselors spoke, they revealed their professional credentials, schooling us in what addiction is and the latest evidence-based practices to treat it. But as I listened, it became clear that most of them had a more personal understanding of addiction. Almost inevitably, they would reveal that they had lived it themselves. They were success stories in recovery.

The stories we heard that weekend were heart-crushing and authentic and inspiring. We learned that we were not alone, and neither was Harry. Our son was not a bad person, he was suffering from a disease. And sadly, ours was not the saddest story.

Living in the dorm were a range of young men in the throes of addiction, arrested in their maturity like Harry. One, a St. Joseph's Prep alum and college graduate, had come back a second time after relapse. Another had spiraled into drug use after his older brother's death from overdose, while a third had been sent here after killing a stranger in a DUI. Looking around the room, I knew from the statistics that not all of these men would survive. My gravest fear, of course, was that Harry would be one of them.

Somehow, the young women in the facility had it even worse. Too often, their stories—their lives—included the agonies of sexual assault and prostitution, often at the hands of drug dealers or boyfriends. Many had been arrested and incarcerated in an ignorant and unsympathetic legal system. I had no daughters, but the pain of these girls and their parents reminded me that my pain could not compare.

I felt nothing but sorrow and empathy toward the other patients. Gone were my judgments of other parents' kids as being the bad element, the corrupt influence on my child. They were all God's children, but addiction had stripped them of so much. All I could think was: Pray. Pray for them all.

I'll never forget one of the first exercises we did that week. The counselor leading the session told us that we needed to adjust to the idea of our child being labeled an addict. That that's who they were.

"Addict." The word stuck with me. It sounded both honest and harsh.

I'm someone who loves language, who thinks about the beauty or ugliness of a phrase. I love words, lyrical or lethal, and despise euphemisms that blunt the harsh pain of truth.

But in that session with Harry, I felt conflicted. I appreciated "addict" for its brutal honesty, yet the word seemed flawed, loaded with judgment and scorn. Compare that with "cancer," which is brutal in its truth without leaving the stain of judgment.

My son is an addict. Harry is an addict. That was hard to say, hard to swallow. But it was the truth. And the truth was the most important thing to me now.

For now, I would claim the truth—*Harry is an addict*—while searching for a more perfect word.

HARRY

I dreaded family weekend. After working so hard to hide my drug use from my parents and brothers, I hated the idea of my two worlds colliding. Rehab Harry and Family Harry were about to be confronted with each other. With the truth.

Over the last couple of weeks, I had watched my peers' relatives come in for the family education program. The counselors spent the weekend educating families on the psychology of addiction and recovery. Then, at the end of the program, the patients would present a time line of their drug use in dramatic detail, having drawn it out on a large posterboard in preparation for the visit. They told it all, from marijuana to heroin to whatever else they might have tried.

When I saw the shocked, saddened faces of their mothers, fathers, and siblings, I panicked. I was certain my family didn't need all of the details. Plus, if I told them the full extent of my using, there was no way in hell I'd be allowed to go back home in a few short days. I didn't realize the exercise might be intended for me more than for my family.

In rehab, people will often "war-story," a verb for how someone talks about the chaos they've experienced in addiction. The robberies, the guns, the blackouts, the greatest scores. When I war-storied, it wasn't because I wanted to be the coolest kid in rehab. I did it because that was how I'd always built my identity. In my eyes, all I had were my war stories. They defined me. Made me hard, street smart. If I let them go, I was letting go of myself.

The problem was, I hadn't learned to share the same version of myself in different areas of my life. The Harry that my parents knew was different from the one that my girlfriend got to know. Even the Harry that my peers in rehab knew was different from the one my counselors got to see.

I wasn't ready to be honest, so I drew out my time line based on the details I assumed my parents already knew. Alcohol: Of course. Marijuana: Yes—the drug tests had been crystal clear on that. Painkillers: They were how I wound up in this place, so I might as well disclose them too. Cocaine: I mentioned that I had tried it, attempting to add some level of surprise and make my parents see this as a detailed and honest assessment. As for everything else—the Xanax, acid, mushrooms, molly, and various other pills that I had taken without even asking what they were—I figured these were better left unspoken. I had already agreed to go to rehab, after all. Did any of this matter? I needed to look better than my peers in my parents' eyes. I needed to get back home.

As I presented my time line, my counselor prodded me to give more. To open up and be honest. He had heard me share many more details among my peers. But now that my parents were sitting in front of me, I couldn't. I wanted to believe my time line. I wasn't ready for my worlds to collide.

After three weeks in rehab, I thought I had become a man. Among my family, I realized that day, I still felt like a child.

MAD

During one of our family exercises, we were asked to write our fears on a whiteboard with an erasable marker. *A little cheesy*, I thought as the exercise started. PJ, the boys, and I took turns writing out our list—relapse, arrests, stealing, sickness, flunking out of school, never having a job, fighting. But as the space filled up on our whiteboard, I hesitated. These streaky, rainbow-colored words were the things we had fought over for years, but they did not capture the depth of my fears for Harry. And so, feeling scared and reluctant, I wrote one last word at the top of our list: death.

That was the truth. Deep down, I was afraid Harry was going to die. I cannot tell you how hard it was to write that word— I felt as though putting it in writing might make it happen. I was scared to death.

As hard as this was for all of us, it was powerful knowing that we were in it together. We started as a family spinning outward with differing perspectives. Now, here we were, through Harry, being pulled back together. For the first time, we were seeing clearly, understanding the truth.

One of our final tasks at Caron was a set of meetings where we would learn of Harry's progress and the challenges he would face after leaving the twenty-eight-day program. It was a time for parents—for PJ and me—to hear the truth. I felt afraid. Harry was supposed to tell us the stories we hadn't been ready for two weeks earlier.

Could I handle it? One truth I was afraid of was heroin. Had Harry used it? As he went through his time line for us, I kept my ears open for that word. When Harry revealed he had not succumbed to using heroin—in large part because he stole from us to keep buying the more expensive drugs—I felt myself relax.

Why did that feel like relief to me? What in God's name was the difference?

As Harry went on with his presentation, there was another concern. I worried he wasn't being completely honest. The revelations he shared weren't as shocking as the ones the other families were learning. His stories seemed polished, as though he was putting on a show. While I knew there was some honesty in it, Harry's time line seemed streamlined, sanitized—too similar to the storytelling he had done at home. We were making progress, but it was clear: Our work in recovery was not yet done.

HARRY

As my month at Caron neared its end, I was faced with the realization that I might not be heading straight home. My counselor scheduled what should have been one of our final individual sessions. Knowing that this would give me clarity on my next steps, I was nervous. Would I be sent away longer? Or would they finally let me out of the program?

I walked into his office with my head held high, exuding confidence. I needed him to see that I was ready. I sat down in my usual spot, a chair closest to his neatly organized desk, adorned with a small photo showing only a minimal glimpse into his personal life. We jumped right in and ran through my experience of the family program, trying to digest what had happened. I replied to his questions with an optimistic spin, trying to show how much I had grown in just a month. Then he told me that the clinical team had made their decision about my aftercare plan. "It is our clinical recommendation that you stay in longer-term treatment," he said.

I was furious. "How long?"

"At least ninety days," he said.

Ninety days. With those words, my show of good behavior fell apart.

"You don't fucking know me," I screamed. "I have a kid. How the hell do you expect me to be away that long?"

"I'm concerned that you aren't taking this seriously," he said. "If you really want to be the father that you talk about, you need to prioritize your recovery."

"You already told me what I have to do. Go to meetings, get a sponsor. I know what I have to do, now it's time to do it. This is bullshit."

I was livid, unloading on him. But the counselor replied matter-of-factly.

"You say you are serious about your recovery, and you would do anything to stay clean. But your actions don't give me confidence that you would succeed if you went straight home. You haven't been honest—with me, with your family, and most important, with yourself."

I stood up and stormed toward the exit. "Fuck this," I yelled, slamming the door behind me.

I couldn't believe it. The counselor had my parents wrapped around his finger, so I knew they would go along. *Ninety more days.* I was pissed. But as I ran through the last four weeks, the longest four weeks of my life, in my head, I couldn't help wondering if he was right. Should I have been more concerned? Did the counselor truly not know me, or had he seen enough addicts like me that my lies and manipulation couldn't fool him?

If he didn't know me, it wasn't for lack of trying. I had resisted opening up to him, afraid that anything I told the staff might make its way back to my family. In that moment, I was overcome by a realization: Though I had been honest in asking for help on the day I came to treatment, I hadn't really been honest since I walked through these doors.

During active addiction, I had built walls around myself—protecting me from exposure, pain, and abandonment. Yet these same walls were now working against me. There was so much I hadn't told my parents—or anyone, for that matter. I had lost my grip on what was true and what I had fabricated.

As I thought over the counselor's words, I was terrified by the idea that I might not have any idea who Harry was. There were still skeletons in the closet, and secrets under the bed, that I wasn't ready to expose.

MAD

There have always been many layers to Harry. It's one of the things I love most about him. But it's also difficult: You're constantly finding things you never wanted to know.

One day while Harry was at Caron, I found a collection of guns under his bed. "Shit!" I screamed. "You've got to be kidding me. In our home? With our granddaughter right here?"

Harry had developed a love of guns years earlier. He would go hunting and target shooting with his uncles, and he enjoyed arguing with me over the Second Amendment. That was the extent of it, as far as I knew. He promised me that he kept his guns in a locker at his uncle's house, and that he used them only for hunting. But the ones under his bed clearly weren't that. I found handguns, revolvers, and a large tan bag containing an AR-15. Nothing you'd use to hunt pheasants with your uncle. Just like his drug use, it was clear I had no understanding of his obsession with guns. Why did he have them? Where did he get them? What were they for? Yet another blunt truth we learned that week.

PJ collected the guns and went with our next door neighbor

to sell them. They drove to someplace in Bensalem, just north of us in Bucks County, and returned home laughing at themselves: two middle-aged suburban dads walking through the door of the gun shop not knowing how to even say "Hi, we have guns to sell." They stammered their way through the transaction and returned home looking giddy and relieved. All I wanted was for the guns to be gone legally, and for us to have written proof.

Firearms aside, we saw good signs in Harry as his twenty-eight days at Caron came to an end. We visited on weekends, bringing Aubrey with us. It was a joy to watch Harry and his daughter together, even if it was brief. Harry's fitfulness subsided, and his defense of nonsense outbreaks by some of his dormmates fizzled. He was ready to move on.

But to where? PJ and Harry's girlfriend pushed for home. I thought they were nuts, and so did Harry's counselor. Opioid addiction takes a lot longer to heal. It's not a "twenty-eight days and we're good" kind of thing.

Once we got over the calendar, we had to tackle the geography. I wanted Harry to stay at Caron and enter the mixed adult male program in the grand manor house that I had stayed in as a kid. But it was incredibly expensive, and *not* where Harry wanted to go. Another option was Caron's program in Florida, designed specifically for young men and women. But that would not work. Too far for a young father with a one-year-old daughter living in the Philadelphia suburbs.

Around this time, another recommendation came our way: Little Creek, a halfway house near Scranton. It was a ninety-day program for young men that would offer Harry discipline and yet a touch of independence. A place to grow. The counselors would teach them how to make their beds, clean the toilets, pitch in at mealtime. I was jealous. That's what I had hoped to teach my boys—caring about your surroundings. No such luck.

I didn't like the idea of Harry going two more hours away to seek treatment. As a state representative, I knew that this area of Pennsylvania was a world of devastation from opioids and heroin. It was my friend Lucille who straightened me out again. Her son had gone to Little Creek and had done well. It was a good place, she told me. Reluctantly, I gave up the center I knew and trusted for Little Creek—for Harry.

Off he went. He was angry that he had to go, but ultimately understood that he needed to. Maybe it helped that he was going to a place I hadn't chosen.

TEN

———

LEARNING TO LIVE

HARRY

As my twenty-eight-day rehab ended, I was faced with reality. The only way to appease my counselor and parents would be to go to a structured sober living home for an additional ninety days of treatment. It sounded like suicide for my relationship with my girl-friend, who was less than eager for me to spend another three months away while she cared for our daughter, alone. But I realized that although I had hidden behind the drugs and my ability to sur-vive the chaos, I was far less capable of living than I believed. I liked the structure, having my day planned out by the minute, with no real responsibilities. Was I really unwilling to listen to the profes-sionals who might know a little more about this disease than I did?

Around this time, a CA named John encouraged me. John was in recovery himself, and he seemed happy with his life. I saw how he arrived at work on time and listened when people spoke. I trusted him. His beliefs came from experience—not just in using, but more important, in learning not to use anymore. And I remembered something that he often told me when I complained about aftercare: "Everyone in treatment should get at least ninety days. Thirty isn't enough. If someone is willing to offer you that, you better take it if you want to give yourself the best chance."

And so, on the morning of my discharge, I woke before sunrise with my bags already packed. In that moment, I cared only about one thing: getting a cigarette. For thirty days, I had craved the warm sensation of nicotine rushing into my lungs. I could still taste the last one I'd had. The morning in the gazebo felt like an eternity ago, separated by many sleepless nights, emotional pain, and the realization that I was afflicted with the disease of addiction.

I thought of what Father Bill had told me: "You're not a bad person trying to be good, you're a sick person trying to get well." I hoped he was right.

As we drove off the campus in a white van, I begged the driver to stop at the first possible gas station so that I could get cigarettes and a coffee. He obliged, and I came out of the store with a twenty-four-ounce coffee and two packs of Newport 100s. Standing in front of the gas station, I lit my first cigarette and was overcome with a sense of calm as the smoke entered my lungs. The sun was just starting to rise on the cold December morning. I missed this. I had missed so much.

MAD

PJ and I visited Little Creek often. At first, we went as concerned parents looking for a sense of what this place could teach our son—then as believers who had seen what this place could contribute to Harry's health and future. In particular, I loved the tattoo-covered rabbi whose mission was helping the young men at Little Creek. Rabbi Mark led several meetings with parents. He could be mean, even brutal, in his assessments of the young men there. The rabbi was quick to call out nonsense, squashing the equivocations that Harry and his housemates used to explain away their problems.

At one point, a one young man proclaimed he had outgrown the place after a week or two. "I got this, Rabbi," he said.

"If you 'got this,'" the rabbi said, "you wouldn't have come back here so soon after your last relapse."

Little Creek offered painful truth-telling when we needed it most. I liked the unlikely rabbi. Harry did, too.

HARRY

Three hours after leaving Caron, I arrived at Little Creek, a large log cabin at the end of a long driveway in the woods. A handful of guys were standing on a side patio smoking cigarettes. They greeted me, and I lit a Newport as I introduced myself, covering all of the important aspects of who I was: I'm Harry, from the Philadelphia area, coming from Caron, was hooked on opiates. That was all I needed to fit right in.

The owner, Andy, and his wife, Barb, greeted me at the door. They were warm and welcoming as they showed me around the house, introducing me to the staff and other residents. After a couple brief conversations, they brought me to my room and left me to unpack. This would be my home for the next ninety days.

My roommate was a guy I knew from Caron. When he saw me, he was surprised, thinking I might have been able to weasel my way out of aftercare and go straight home. I had only known him a few weeks, but seeing him was comforting.

Before coming here, I was told that if I behaved well—participating in groups, following the rules, and keeping up with my daily chores—I would be able to go home on a pass for Christmas. I had already missed Thanksgiving with my daughter, so that was one of the things that sold me on coming: the idea that in time,

I would have a chance to earn back some of the privileges of a normal life. If the first couple weeks went well, I could get a cellphone (though not one with Internet), and people could start visiting me every weekend. I got lost in daydreams, picturing myself reconnecting with friends. Most of all, I thought about how my girlfriend and daughter would be able to see me here.

The house had a structured routine. We attended group meetings during the day and ate meals together in the dining room. Every night, we would help clean up before heading off to a 12-step meeting in the area. There was very little down time, except for on Sundays, when families came to visit. Keeping busy was fine with me. In my free time, I often fantasized about going home on the Christmas pass and never returning. If I played it right, maybe my parents would see that I was ready—that I was done with treatment.

A few days in, a counselor pulled me and a couple of other guys aside. We sat around the large leather couches in the main room on the first floor, wondering if we were in trouble. "The reason I've got you guys together is to tell you about one of the guys that you were in Caron with. Do you remember Sam?" he asked. Of course we did. We had just seen him days ago.

"Sam passed away yesterday, of an overdose."

I was shocked. It couldn't be true. I had just seen Sam. He was taking this whole recovery thing so seriously. Sam, the quiet boy whose sincere voice offered me hope. He had signed my copy of the *Narcotics Anonymous Basic Text* the night before I left. In rehab, we all signed each other's books, leaving our phone numbers and promising that we'd get together once we'd completed treatment. Sam told me his plans: He would go home for a few days, ignoring his aftercare recommendation until after the holidays, then check in to a halfway house. We later learned that he was found in his pickup truck less than twenty-four hours after coming home from treatment.

Of all the people at Caron, I never thought it would be him. The news was shocking, overwhelming, sobering. What would have happened if I'd gone home myself?

Around that time, we started meeting with a rabbi named Mark. I had never known a rabbi before, and this guy didn't fit my mental picture. He was covered in tattoos. He was a large, gruff man— quick to call us out if we got out of line—but he had such a warm heart that it was easy to open up. In one of our first groups, he talked about prayer. I was immediately turned off. Praying always seemed like a sign of weakness, something people do when they can't figure things out on their own. But as I listened to Mark, I couldn't help being interested. Unlike the priests and nuns of my childhood, he talked about prayer in a scientific way. He explained that the act of speaking creates brain furrows in a way that can literally change the chemistry of one's mind. Seeking help through prayer goes deeper than any God we can understand. He told us, "You don't need to believe in order for it to work." That was my opening.

"I want you to try something," Mark told us. He asked us to close our eyes. As we sat around a table, eyes closed, some of the guys began to laugh—a way of coping with the uncomfortable silence. But when everyone fell silent again, Mark yelled a curse word. I can't remember which, but it doesn't matter. It had its intended effect. The entire room broke out laughing, unable to comprehend how this was in any way therapeutic.

"You see the power of saying something out loud?" he asked. He explained that without us seeing or feeling anything, his voice had the power to both startle us and make us laugh. Praying out loud had this same effect, he said. When you see something, and say it out loud, you are also hearing it. It's far more powerful than simply thinking it in your mind. Which is exactly what each of us needed. A new way of thinking.

Later that night, still suspicious, I thought I would give the whole prayer thing a try. I went into the bathroom, turned on the shower, and set the faucet running. Finding privacy in a house full of twenty other addicts is tough, and I was far too embarrassed to let anyone hear me pray. But I pushed through. Barely louder than the running water, I muttered the first prayer that I could think of.

"God, help me."

That was it. I didn't know what else to say, but as I sat in the bathroom, I knew for certain that I needed help—more than I had been willing to ask for. The ridiculousness of hiding in the bathroom to pray wasn't lost on me. I thought of all of the times I had been so high or drunk that I'd blacked out, vomited, or woken up naked in a stranger's home. For some reason, none of those moments had felt as embarrassing as what I was doing now: praying for help, in a house full of drug addicts.

"God, help me." The words brought me back to the hopeless nights holding my daughter in her nursery. Perhaps I had been praying all along, disguising it as conversation with an infant. More important, maybe my prayers had been answered.

MAD

I was excited when we learned Harry would get two or three days at home for Christmas. A chance to have him back under our roof, to celebrate the joy of Christmas with Aubrey, who was growing and becoming her own person, confident and smart and happy. Her innocence and joy brought us such delight.

And yet I worried. How would the brief visit go? Who would Harry see and connect with? How would he handle the holidays and all the festivities—all the drinking that goes with celebrating in our lives? I had just tissue-paper-thin confidence in what we were doing.

Nervous, I asked him: Should I remove all alcohol from the house? Should Christmas be dry? I was willing.

Harry said no. Alcohol in the house was not his problem.

I didn't know how Harry felt about the visit. Would he try to convince us that he didn't need to go back to treatment? That he was ready to be home permanently? There was the urgency of Aubrey, of his daughter. But in the bottom of my heart, I knew that Aubrey would be all right, surrounded by love. Cutting Harry's treatment short would put her in the greatest danger, danger of losing her father for good.

Harry was not even sixty days into recovery. *We* were not even sixty days into recovery. It was all new—precarious, fragile.

As Harry came in the back door, duffel bag in hand, he looked like a soldier returning from war. I was struck by how good he looked. The color of his face and skin had returned. His smile was back—a cautious smile.

Still, for the entire two-day visit, I fretted over his every move. Had he been in his room too much today? Was he going out the back door too much? Staying in the bathroom a little too long? Cigarettes were no longer my worry. I let that go. Still, I know I watched him too closely, tiptoeing through the holidays.

I wondered how others would see him, and even more, how he would see himself among our family and friends. That worry was a waste of time. Our friends and family were fantastic: so happy for Harry and his return to health. Harry had always been a magnet to people, and the same went for the aunts and uncles, cousins and neighbors. To a person, they celebrated and supported him.

My eldest brother, Bob, in particular, told Harry how proud he was of him, that he was doing something most of us might never be able to do. While relatives tended to see Pat as the golden boy in our family, Bob saw in Harry a strength and success that surpassed Pat's remarkable accomplishments. And my sister, Maryann. So positive. So supportive. A faithful letter writer.

The two and a half days went fast, a blur. Then, just as quickly as he arrived, Harry went back. No big fight. I was relieved.

HARRY

Before coming home on Christmas Eve, I secretly hoped that I would convince my mom and dad to let me stay for good. But something happened when I actually got there. Something I hadn't expected.

I quickly realized that I felt more comfortable in rehab than I did in my own house. Being home was like torture. There were some positives, of course, like seeing my family and especially my daughter. But as I looked around the house, all I remembered was the pain I'd felt when I last lived there. Every surface in every bathroom had once been a place where I snorted lines. I had been so creative. Every hard, flat surface was fair game for crushing pills. I felt tempted to run my finger along the top of the toilet tank, checking for white or blue residue. The drugs had given me the ability to deal with life. Without them, I wasn't sure how to cope.

At Little Creek, I was making progress with the routine. Waking up on time for morning group—always sure to save enough time for a cigarette. Making my bed, doing the dishes, going to meetings, and most important, not doing drugs. Now I was back home for two days, navigating my roles as a brother, son, father, and boyfriend. All of them loaded with expectations I imagined I had to tiptoe around. It didn't make me want to use drugs, but it made me want to run away, back to the safety of treatment. Away from expectations.

The irony almost made me laugh. At Caron, I had been desperate to leave treatment after twenty-eight days. Now, two months in, I was terrified to come home.

MAD

Harry went back to Little Creek, and time seemed to speed up. I was eager for him to come home, get some independence, find friends, and start building a new social life. He would go back to being a father—a healthy one, I hoped. But how?

We were all met with a series of decisions: What was next? Where would Harry go? Home, for sure. But in what kind of arrangement?

"People, places, things." At Caron, we had heard over and over again that if Harry wanted to continue in his recovery, he couldn't return to the habits and circumstances of the past. So I talked with Harry. What did we need to change?

People. Harry needed to come home—home to us—but I worried he would contact his old friends. Mark, for example. He was in prison at this point, and I wondered if Harry would reach out to him out of sympathy, or because he had no one else. Harry assured me, "Mom, I know it's too soon for me to be in touch. I get it."

Things. Harry said we could still drink around him, that alcohol was not his drug of choice. Still, I was skeptical. We have a bar at our house that the boys call the Partisan Pub. Its walls are covered with political pictures and memorabilia from Pat's six years of work in the Obama White House. Today, with the photos from all of my campaigns and our family's support for candidates at every level, the walls of the small room have run out of space.

In the small kitchenette behind the bar, there were three narrow shelves holding bottles of booze—from gin and Jack Daniel's to cognac and cases of red wine. That worried me. I had a bright idea, something I'd seen bar and restaurant owners do to try to prevent theft. (Turns out I was wrong again: The practice prevents fruit flies, not theft.) I thoughtfully wrapped the cap of each bottle with Saran Wrap, thinking that would do the trick. Of course, this was useless, ignorant. The thin sheets of plastic did nothing but transparently expose my panic.

Places. How could Harry avoid all the old places that had led to his using? I fought against having him return to work at PJ's company, worried that Harry would find his way back to drug use, just as he'd done when he last worked there. I figured it was time to start something new. PJ disagreed.

From the beginning of our relationship, something that drew me to PJ was his optimism. On one of our first dates, driving in one of his famously beat-up cars, we were late getting home because we got a flat tire. As we pulled off on the shoulder of Cheltenham Avenue, all I could think was, "What a lousy place to get a flat." I didn't say those words, but I was surprised by what PJ did say: "What a fantastic spot to get a flat. This broad shoulder by the side of the road, and all?" He changed our tire, and we were on our way

That's PJ—ever the optimist. Whatever the circumstance he sees the good first. By bringing Harry back to the company, he was giving him another chance under his roof. That job at the bicycle company would be Harry's broad shoulder.

We were parents seeing through different lenses, relearning to live with our adult son. Learning the ways of recovery, learning the steps.

HARRY

Things weren't going well with my girlfriend. Our trust had been shattered when my drug use came to light, and my decision to stay in treatment became a point of constant conflict. I had left her to care for our daughter all by herself, and I struggled to articulate why I'd stayed in treatment, afraid to risk leaving. As my ninety days at Little Creek came to an end, I was faced with the realization that it likely wouldn't work out between us.

Piece by piece, the future I envisioned had been picked apart.

Within three years, I had dropped out of college, had a child, and spent months living in a structured sober living home in the middle of nowhere. Now, topping it all off, my hope of raising a child together as a couple—with parents who were both present, just like I had been raised—was slipping away. I was becoming the dad I never wanted to be. I wasn't there.

I decided to do something I generally didn't do. I asked for help. I discussed what was happening with my peers, the counselors, the rabbi, anyone who would listen. The resounding response was always the same: Focus on your recovery above all else. If I started using again, I would lose the opportunity to be a father, a son—or anything else, for that matter. It would no longer be my decision. It was a sobering thought, but it carried with it the possibility that maybe, just maybe, I could build a new life. It was time to stop dreaming of "getting my life back." I was going to create a new one.

Each night at Little Creek, we attended 12-step meetings, loading into two identical white vans and making our way to one of the local groups. At first I wasn't sure I'd buy into the program, but attendance was required in the house.

When we started going, the thing that surprised me most was the people. These weren't just gatherings of older white men with drinking problems. Perhaps I have seen too many movies. From my very first meeting, the room teemed with people from every walk of life. Young and old, rich and poor.

As I listened to people share their stories, something became clear. My mind. I was able to stop thinking about myself and my problems, if only for a few minutes. It was a feeling of reprieve that I never knew I needed.

There is a common expression about addicts and alcoholics. We are described as "egomaniacs with low self-esteem"—which, if you think about it, is an exhausting combination. To focus on yourself and only yourself all of the time, but always in a negative light. For years, a never-ending stream of worst-case scenarios had played out in my head, prompting preemptive lies and excuses. I always stayed at-the-ready, and it kept me from ever being present in the moment.

I could clearly hear the insanity when others shared. Rambling on about anything and everything from relationship troubles to road rage. Men and women opened up about the craziest thoughts that popped into their minds. Some were sad, some hilarious, but all of them showed the courage to be honest with the group. I quickly realized that these people thought exactly the way I did. No matter what they looked like, how different we were in circumstance or appearance, or whether they were from my generation or that of my grandparents, we had the same condition. We were bound in likeness through our shared pain, but many of them had turned their pain into hope and joy.

I was fueled by their stories, by their progress—and even by my own. By the end of those three months, I started to feel better physically, emotionally, and spiritually. My withdrawal symptoms were nearly gone, and I was learning to love myself again. Things, for the first time in a long time, were good. I had real friends who cared about me, all of us living in the safe bubble of that house outside of Scranton.

But I was about to leave. Who would I be then?

ELEVEN

DROPS AND BUCKETS

Home is the place where, when you have to
go there, they have to take you in.

—ROBERT FROST

HARRY

February 28, 2013. I had counted down to this moment for a hundred and twenty-two days, but when the morning actually came, it crept up on me after a peaceful sleep. As I rose from bed, I felt like I was in a movie, watching myself from the outside. The walls of the facility, which had felt like the confines of a prison at first, were about to fall away. As I made my way to morning group, I felt so light, so ready for the next chapter—my real life.

At morning check-in, I told the group how nervous I was to leave the safety of Little Creek, but how grateful I was for the support of the house and the foundation and the relationships I had built. I tried to encourage the newer guys to really give this program a chance.

Then I went over the plans for my long-term recovery with the clinical team. By now, I had the language down. I would go to meetings, get a sponsor, build a network of support in recovery. And of course I would avoid the people, places, and things of my past, replacing them with a new way of life. I was ready.

But first I needed to go through the discharge protocol. Answering questions, going through exit interviews with the staff, and some lighter conversations, recalling how difficult I had been when I first arrived. We joked about the pranks I'd played, about my disdain for morning yoga and the freezing cold hikes they would make us take through the snow. The staffers had truly become my family. Another new family.

As we sat in the office, a counselor pulled my belongings from a locked cabinet. There was a large Ziploc bag containing my wallet, iPhone, and other items that had been withheld throughout my stay. My eyes landed on the phone, adorned in a Magpul firearm accessory branded case. It was dead from lack of use, so I plugged it in and waited for the small white apple to appear onscreen.

The counselor sat with me as the phone started up. He was there to help me go through the contacts, to delete and block the numbers of drug dealers and old friends who might try to drag me down. I neglected to mention that the numbers of my drug dealers were stored in my brain, not my phone. I had been afraid to save their numbers. Names like Money, DeZ, and Dolla would have been hard to explain if someone was looking through my contact list.

As my phone illuminated with power, I waited for the messages to pour in. Who had been calling, texting? Who had been wondering where I was? I thought often about my friends, wondering if anyone else had gotten treatment. Who of my friends were still stuck in the cycle?

After a moment, a notification popped up on the screen: 3 TEXT MESSAGES. That was it. What a disappointing display.

"I'm good," read the first message, from DeZ. It was code, letting me know that he had pills for sale. He'd always been my most reliable dealer.

"HAR . . . ARE YOU ALIVE?" read a message from Nikki, one of my friends' girlfriend. *A reasonable question,* I thought.

The final message was from Marge, one of my co-workers, a motherly figure from the office. "I am praying for you, Harry" was all she said.

My ego was crushed. Where the hell was everyone? For four months, I had been going through the most important experience of my life. Yet the friends I had once felt such profound loyalty toward hadn't even bothered to reach out. No one seemed to have noticed I was gone.

It reinforced that the lessons I'd been taught in recovery were right. I did need to find new people. But as I prepared to head home in a few short hours, I knew that the places—my home and work—weren't going to change anytime soon. As for things: My guns had been sold, so my only non-drug-related hobby was also gone.

That evening, my dad came to pick me up after getting off work. My bags were packed: an orange backpack, a trash bag for the extra clothing I had accumulated, and a large brown envelope holding all of the letters I'd received while I was away. Life at home would be different. I would no longer be able to hide out in the safety of a treatment center, where I could process my reactions in groups of my peers. I would have to dive in and start living my life again. Would the principles I'd been taught be enough?

We drove home in uncomfortable silence. So much had happened since I last sat here with my dad, yet there was so little to say. Where would we even start? I could sense his worry, the question of whether this whole thing would work. Was there anything he could do? He had given me so much. All I could do was try to reassure him that I would give this everything I had.

MAD

Harry taught me an expression recently: "You earn trust in drops and pour it away in buckets."

Could we trust him again? When Harry came home, that was

the biggest question. Over the past few years, Harry had lied to us, stolen from us, failed us in countless ways. All leading up to that day in the bank when our buckets of trust poured away. Now, through the fog, I strained to think of a day in our future when we would trust each other again.

I remember feeling as if recovery had taken us 122 steps ahead—and yet important steps back. We had gone from Harry telling us nothing about his life, or lying about his comings and goings, to this new scenario in which he had to ask permission for the smallest things. "Can I use the car to go to a meeting?" "I'm going to meet up with my sponsor. Is that okay?" Still, I beamed as Harry made his way home with PJ. We were baby-stepping our way back into Harry's adulthood.

The day of his return reminded me of the buzz of excitement in my childhood home when my brother Bob came back from Vietnam. Our family had gone as a gang to the airport—this was in the 1960s, when you could walk right up to the gate—and met him holding up placards that said WELCOME HOME, WE MISSED YOU.

We didn't do that for Harry on the day he returned from treatment. It felt like too much. But that's how I felt. Harry was our returning soldier.

HARRY

When I stepped through the doorway, I was welcomed by the familiar smell of home. An aroma of wood and dust that triggered the memories of first visiting this house when my parents bought it ten years earlier. As I looked around, the house was entirely unchanged. Well, almost. For one thing, my room had been rearranged slightly. The bed now faced in a different direction, and the desk had been moved to the opposite corner.

The second change was in the bar downstairs. The bottles were still in place, one for every category of spirit. But now, a coating of Saran Wrap had been wound around each bottle—to protect me from relapse, I supposed. I laughed to myself, thinking of the lengths I'd gone to score: stealing, climbing through windows of houses. My mom had always sought control over my choices, a reality that never quite existed. How many times in high school had I snuck drinks from these bottles and replaced the missing liquor with water? Had anyone even opened them since then? I envisioned someone at a political fund-raiser ordering Cognac only to receive a watered down, disgusting drink.

As I settled in that weekend, something else was different in the house—something I had known would be the hardest. My girlfriend and daughter were gone. We had decided to end our relationship while I was away, and she now lived with her aunt. The empty nursery was a sobering image of the damage my addiction had done. The room was stocked with books and toys, yet there was no child there to play with them.

My daughter was nearly eighteen months old, and I had either been high or institutionalized through it all. In treatment, I had about thirty pictures of her that I carried with me. In those four months, she had grown so much, learning new things every day. She was different now, and so was I. We would need to start over.

The phrase from treatment, "gained in drops and lost in buckets," rang out in my head as I stared at the baby's empty room.

MAD

I worried about Harry making new friends. He had always been the most social of our kids. How would he fare without the people of his past? Where do you go at twenty-two to find new friends, ones you can trust?

I knew very little about 12-step meetings. We learned about them at Caron and Little Creek, and we had the opportunity to sit in on some of the clinical groups. But I didn't know much about the day-to-day meetings that would fill Harry's weeks at home.

Once, years before, I had attended an AA group with a family member who was giving up drinking and wanted a little extra support. It felt foreign, as though I had walked into the wrong class on the first day of school. The meeting was part social gathering— light conversation over coffee—and part therapy. I heard person after person begin in the usual way. "Hi, my name is Sarah, and I'm an alcoholic." Some speakers said they were new to recovery, while others had years under their belts. Each story was heartfelt and heart-delivered. And they all held something else: naked truth. One woman had come back after a relapse. I admired her courage, her willingness to expose her regrets to others.

As I listened, I could not help looking inward, knowing I did not have that strength—the strength to so clearly, publicly state my own brokenness. "Hi, my name is Madeleine, and I'm an angry, worried, broken mother." "Hi, Mad," they would say back, welcoming me.

Now, years later, I timidly asked Harry when and where his meetings took place. Harry said he'd tried a handful of local AA and NA meetings and quickly found that the AA meetings were less helpful. An alcoholic's journey was different from his, he said. Harry also traveled farther, to meetings in South Philadelphia or Bucks County—each with different audiences on different nights. A bit like Goldilocks, Harry was testing this one and that, meeting new people and seeing which group might fit. One night, I asked if I could go with him. He gently told me no. It was not my place. It was his place.

Whenever Harry left for a meeting, I worried. A couple of times, I even followed him to a local chapter that I knew of, sheepishly driving by thirty minutes later—just to see if I might catch sight of him standing outside in the dark with the others, smoking, a coffee cup in hand.

Many of these meetings took place in communities that I

knew had been hit hard by addiction and overdose. As a state representative, I received a Significant Criminal Activity report every Friday, which listed assaults, car thefts, and burglaries along with the number of overdose saves and deaths in my local district. When I saw this report, my first reaction was to recommend that the reporting for overdose victims not be categorized as "significant criminal activity." Second, I noticed that too many of the lives saved and lost were in the towns near the one where we lived. For years, I had thought the problem was our family's—that the fire was in our house. Turns out it was a statewide, and increasingly countrywide, crisis.

There's a story from my father's life that always comes back when I think about my worries for my kids or the people I serve in politics. When my dad was a boy and entered high school—North Catholic High in Philadelphia—he left all his friends to travel by bus and trolley to a new school in the city, a foreign place to a kid who'd grown up in the suburbs. He knew no one. As he stood alone in the cafeteria on the first day of school, short and shy and nervous, another boy walked up. He was much bigger than my dad, likely an upperclassman.

"Hey, kid, do you know anyone?" he said.

"No," my father replied.

"Then stand next to me."

With that, my father's nervousness was lifted—if for only a moment—as the two stood together in silence, the older boy letting him know he was not alone.

I thought about that story in those months when Harry worked to rebuild his life. Who would stand by him? Even in silence? Maybe especially in silence?

HARRY

The night after coming home, I went out to a meeting. I had prepared a list of groups for every night of the week, to keep me from having the excuse of not being able to find one. It was the first time I'd driven a car by myself since rehab. I missed driving, the freedom of being able to go anywhere I wanted. But the CDs in my car were like a soundtrack to my addiction, so I quickly opted for the radio.

The meeting took place in a clubhouse on our town's main street, a small building flanked by restaurants and shops. I must have driven past hundreds of times without realizing what was going on inside. The front windows had curtains drawn shut to protect the anonymity of the people attending.

Standing outside, I realized how alone I truly was. I didn't know anyone within two hours of me who was working the program. I felt scared. Could I open up to these people? I was afraid of being rejected—but even more afraid of relapsing. So I walked in. Inside, the space opened up to what looked like a living room, with dirty carpeting and rows of folding chairs facing a desk. There was a small kitchen in the back with a large coffeepot, stacks of Styrofoam cups, and a canister of powdered creamer.

Outside, I hadn't talked with anyone. I kept the brim of my hat low and the hood of my sweatshirt up, trying to look as unapproachable as possible. But when the meeting started, I quickly relaxed. A gentleman at the desk opened with a moment of silence. Then, after reading some 12-step literature, he introduced two speakers to share their stories. They were both older, around my parents' age. I fought the desire to distance myself from them. Someone in the meeting mentioned that people don't end up here because they want to, but because they need to. The voices of my counselors rang in my head, telling me the same thing. That I needed to keep coming back, and I needed to find support.

After a few meetings, I decided to ask one of the members to sponsor me. He looked nothing like me and was twenty-five years older, but when he spoke at the meetings, he conveyed an honesty and confidence that I desired. He seemed content with his own life. More important, he'd been clean for almost twenty years.

When you're new to recovery, asking someone to be your sponsor feels like asking a girl out on a date. You, the drug addict who doesn't know how to live, are supposed to ask someone who has their shit together if you can enter into a relationship in which the two of you will go from not knowing each other to talking every day. The low-self-esteem part of me had me convinced he'd say no.

But one night, as the group stood outside of the meeting smoking cigarettes, I positioned myself near this man. I felt too shy to introduce myself but brave enough to just be there, hoping that if I stood this close for long enough, he would have to say something. And he did. He asked how I was doing, how long had I been coming around. As we talked, I opened up, telling him I'd just gotten home from treatment and was trying to dive in to the program. When I finally got the courage to ask him to sponsor me, he said yes without hesitation.

Now I had a sponsor—but I still had no friends, and he sensed that.

"I sponsor this other guy that I want you to reach out to," he said. "His name is Jack, and he can introduce you to a lot of other guys your age to get you plugged in." He gave me Jack's number and suggested I get in touch.

When your sponsor makes a suggestion, you're supposed to take it. It's like being "suggested" to pull your parachute ripcord when you're skydiving. It could be something small, like sitting in the front row of a meeting, or a bigger ask, like staying out of a relationship for your first year. Either way, if you don't want to relapse and die, it's probably a good idea to listen.

Later that night, I sat in my room agonizing over the call. I was desperate to stay clean and desperate for friends—but this was hard. What was I supposed to say? "My sponsor gave me your number. Wanna be friends?" I went back and forth. Maybe I should put it off until tomorrow. Maybe I'll see the guy at a meeting. That would be less awkward.

But the desperation of not wanting to use drugs again took hold, and I called.

As the phone rang, regret washed over me. *What am I going to say?*

"Hello?" the guy answered, in a voice so soft I could hardly hear him.

"Hi, I'm Harry," I replied. "Kenny gave me your number."

I waited for him to respond, wondering if I'd used the right code words, the ones that would save me from having to explain who I was or why I was calling. Maybe Kenny had given him a heads-up.

"Hey, what's up, Harry," he said after what felt like an eternity. "I'm going out to eat at TGI Fridays with some guys right now, if you want to come?"

It felt weird. I had called this stranger out of the blue, and now he was inviting me out to eat with two other guys I didn't know. My instinct was to say no, but up to this point, my instincts had led me to a drug-fueled, self-resenting life that I wanted to change.

"Sure," I responded, knowing I would need to ask my parents. For now, that's what progress would have to look like. A twenty-two-year-old asking if he's allowed to go out to dinner.

MAD

One evening Harry asked if he could go to TGI Fridays to meet up with three other young men in recovery. I said yes, but I worried. Were these guys really in recovery? How did we know they weren't old friends? Relapsing is a very real threat for many in treatment and recovery. It's not a moral failing, but the consequences can be fatal.

At the same time—much as I wanted to watch him every second—really, I wanted him out in the world, meeting people. I desperately wanted that for him: friends who would replace the ones he'd left behind.

So I said yes.

HARRY

When I walked into Fridays, Jack waved me over to his table. He was thin, with long hair like the images of Jesus that I'd seen countless times, and a voice that sounded even quieter in person than it had on the phone. The noise level in the restaurant made it almost impossible to understand a word that he said.

Then there was Coles—larger and louder than Jack, with a personality to match. From the way they talked, I could tell that Coles and Jack had known each other for a while, dating back to their own partying in high school. Across from them was T, or Terrence. Coles and Terrence both had a few years clean, and Jack was just coming back from a relapse.

Throughout dinner, the three of them told stories of a recent trip to New York City, when Jack was going through withdrawals and Coles was dragging him around the city. Even then, they managed to have a blast. I sat quietly and listened to their conversation, wondering how I fit into this group. But they welcomed me, even if it felt like I brought nothing to the table.

At the end of dinner, Jack told me he was going to a nearby meeting the next night. He didn't drive, so I offered to take him.

When I went to pick him up, I realized he lived only three houses down from my parents. What were the odds? He got in the car, and neither of us said much, not knowing each other well enough to keep a conversation going. We both seemed happy sitting in silence as we made our way to the meeting. I asked what music he liked, and we realized we had the same taste. So I threw in a CD, and away we went.

We arrived twenty minutes early, so we stood near the entrance and smoked cigarettes with our backs against the wall—still in silence, but comforted in knowing we weren't alone. When the meeting let out, we stood there for another twenty minutes, smoking and leaning against the same wall. Then, with a nod, we both knew it was time to go. On the way home, I asked Jack where he was going tomorrow, and offered to drive again.

Over the course of the next few months, the ritual continued. New CDs, silent rides, and over time, a friendship that started to grow. We were able to pull small pieces of information out of each other. Jack told me about the last time he got clean, and how he fell into a relapse. It came in bits and pieces, but neither of us was in a rush.

Over time, as we stood alone at meetings, people began to come up and talk to us. Like those drops of trust that I was accumulating with my mom, my network of friends in recovery began to grow.

MAD

After deciding AA was not for him, Harry started a new NA meeting in Roslyn, a neighborhood next to ours, with his new friend Jack. Jack is a terrific young man; quiet, understated, with caring eyes and a warm smile, eager to help in subtle ways. He lived with his grandmother down the hill from us—in a three-story Colonial like the one I grew up in—and spent lots of time helping her out around the house. Jack helped his grandmom. Say no more, I liked him instantly. Puzzlingly, yet beautifully, Jack looks like Jesus Christ.

I liked it when Jack would stop in to help Harry, whether it was rearranging Aubrey's room after she and her mother moved away, or working with Harry on his truck. At one point, Harry told us Jack needed a car, so we sold him the bright blue Ford Escape that our good friend Larry had driven before he died. I loved seeing Jack doing so well, driving around in the car Larry had prized.

As different as Harry's new friends were from one another, there was something they all had in common. They were quiet, reserved, as if they shared an experience I could never be a part of. Unlike Harry's friends from active addiction—the ghostly looking ones whose eye contact you could not get—his new friends looked you right in the eye, openly and honestly. Their gaze revealing a compassion and an understanding that surpassed my own.

HARRY

Less than a week after coming home, I went back to work. It felt surreal, being back in the same office, with the same people, sitting at the same desk where I'd spent so many days high or in withdrawal. I worried about who knew what. Did my co-workers know what I'd been doing these last four months? There weren't many reasons why a twenty-two-year-old would take extended medical leave without informing any of his colleagues first. But when I showed up at the office, I found that little had changed. Again, I was welcomed back warmly.

As a customer service rep, I would spend all day on the phone, taking calls from our dealer network and the occasional consumer. I wanted to give it everything that I had, to prove to everyone that I deserved to be there. No longer would I be the boss's son who everyone views in a negative light.

Until this point, I knew that I fit the stereotype. When I left Little Creek, I reviewed the string of messages I had sent my supervisor, explaining why I was late for work: "I got a flat tire." "I'm sick." "My daughter isn't feeling well." "There's a lot of traffic." A new excuse every morning, each of which was obvious bullshit. An honest version of these texts would have read "I'm withdrawing and need to cop before I come in." Or maybe "I got too high last night and overslept."

I wanted work to be the place where I learned how to incorporate honesty and integrity into my life. I would show up on time—early, in fact. If I didn't know how to answer a question, I would ask for help. If I made a mistake, I would take accountability. When things went well, I wouldn't gloat. Small actions, executed perfectly, would be how I'd grow.

One of the first things I did was clean out my workspace. My desk had always been a mess. There were old papers and notes everywhere, so I opened my top drawer—the "junk" drawer—and started rifling through it. When I made it to the bottom, beneath the papers and pens, I found something I didn't expect. A Subox-one.

I froze. I hadn't seen one of those small orange films since the last time I'd used—in the garage in October. My first thought was anger. Why did I have to find this now? How many times had I sat at this desk in withdrawal, waiting for a dealer to respond while my fix was just inches away? Now I'm trying to stay clean, and one magically appears? You never find drugs when you need them.

I ran to the bathroom and flushed it down the toilet. I didn't tell anyone, but as I watched the Suboxone circle the porcelain bowl, I knew something inside me must have changed. The sight of it, which had always brought such peace and joy, now stoked anxiety and fear.

I wondered what might have happened if I'd gone back to work after only twenty-eight days in treatment. Would I have been strong enough to flush it? Or would my habits have gotten the best of me? Would I have shoved it into my mouth before having time to think?

MAD

Benjamin Franklin said "Glass, china, and reputation are easily cracked and never well mended." When Harry came home, I worried that would be the case with us. That even if he regained some of his credibility—drop by drop, repair by repair—the relationship would never fully heal. Would we always see the mended cracks?

Now, as I look back on those first weeks and months, I believe Franklin was wrong. As Harry grew in recovery, the fine china that he was became stronger and more beautiful than before. I trust Harry now more than ever—he is unapologetically honest and transparent.

In that season, there were other changes in the air. No more fighting. No more scared-to-death rants from me. There was peace in our house for the first time in forever. Harry would wake up early looking bright-eyed, disciplined in his work, and committed in his love for Aubrey. I loved hearing him talk with PJ after work, offering ideas and insights and arguments for trying this or changing that at the company. He was engaged in his work, learning from PJ and enjoying it. PJ loved it too.

And one thing more: Harry was trying to quit smoking. He started with vaping, then switched to the patch. I kept quiet, believing this was too much too soon to hope for. But before too long, he had done it. He quit smoking cigarettes, and vaping. He would still enjoy a cigar with PJ once in a while—talking and relaxing behind the house, where Harry used to smoke alone. But that was it. Building and rebuilding bonds in the swirling smoke on our patio.

HARRY

As my involvement in meetings deepened, so too did my relationships. I had my daughter each weekend, and I cherished every moment we shared. We played with dolls, took naps, and colored. We watched movies and danced together. As a toddler she was always on the move, and curious of her surroundings. Getting smarter every day.

I could feel my parents' guard coming down. Not a lot, but little by little. They no longer seemed to worry when I went to the bathroom, wondering if I was using again if I took too long. I spent a lot of time in the basement, reading or watching TV. With each passing day, I heard fewer and fewer footsteps above, the sound of my parents making their way to the door to check on me. Each night, I would tell them what meeting I was attending, then provide a report when I made it home. Each check-in was a new drop in the bucket of trust.

My friend Mariah once told me, "If you want self-esteem, start by doing estimable acts." And so I did. Through my conversations, or my extended silences with Jack, I learned that I could begin to be honest again. It sounds silly, but being truthful is a skill that has to be relearned. It felt unnatural after so many years of lies. I needed to *show* honesty and integrity rather than just talk about them. So if I felt the urge to lie, I learned to just shut up instead.

In those days, weeks, and months, I could see the hope in my mom's eyes each time I returned home from a meeting or work, each instance proving to be a small win for both of us. For so long, I had craved a lack of accountability. Now, I was learning—accountability could save my life.

TWELVE

THE MIRACLE

There is advantage in wisdom
won through pain.

—AESCHYLUS

HARRY

Back in rehab, the counselors had said that if I stayed committed to recovery, holding on to it as my top priority and taking suggestions from my sponsor and new friends, the desire to use would eventually lift. "Don't leave before the miracle happens," they would say. When I first heard this, I considered it complete and utter bullshit. The idea that through some magic, or maybe a so-called higher power, the obsession that had plagued me since my first drink would somehow disappear.

For the first six months, I was right. Even though I wasn't taking drugs, I thought about them constantly. Every new life experience reminded me of a reason I might have used in the past. Feeling happy—use. Sad—use. Birthday party—use. Funeral—use. Stomachache—use. When I got through one of these triggering events without using, it bolstered my ability to experience life without drugs. But the thought was always there. At work, I would be having an unpleasant phone call with an irate consumer and think about how much more tolerable it would be with a small line of Percocet. But in rehab and at meetings, I was taught to "play the tape through" and remind myself where that one line might take me. I knew clearly where it led. Back to the misery of a life consumed by drugs.

During that first year in recovery, 12-step meetings had become an integral part of my life. A place where I was free to be myself—or really, *learn* to be myself for the first time. In the meetings, I no longer had to play the chameleon. I didn't have to hide my past or pretend it never happened. I learned to grow in spite of, and because of, what I'd been through.

In meetings, I learned to listen—not just to hear, but to actively listen to someone else long enough that the inner voice in my head quieted down. The sensation of silence in my head was what I had really wanted all along. The drugs had temporarily given me that peace, a slowing of my thoughts and fears. But it had been a false peace. Now I was learning to quiet those voices and anxieties without drugs.

I found myself doing things I dreaded when I was in rehab. John, the CA at Caron, had talked about hanging out at diners and bowling alleys after 12-step meetings. Having just exited a fast lifestyle filled with drugs, sex, and parties, it didn't exactly sound exciting. But as I met new friends on those nights at TGI Fridays or Applebee's, I found fellowship with people just like me. People who would stay up until midnight or later just to talk. We were helping one another heal.

One evening, as the anniversary of my clean date approached, I was showering before heading out to see some friends at my homegroup, the meeting I had committed to attending every week. As the water washed over me, I suddenly realized that I had gone through the entire day without wanting to use.

I couldn't believe it. Not only had I not felt the desire, I hadn't even thought about drugs at all. As I racked my brain, trying to remember my last craving, I couldn't find it. It had been days, maybe even weeks. The desire had been lifted. And in that moment I realized that the men and women I'd met through the program had been right this whole time.

The miracle had happened.

MAD

One morning, Harry asked me where he could buy a birthday cake. "What for?" I asked.

"A celebration," he said. "Tonight is the first anniversary of our Roslyn homegroup meeting."

I did not speak it out loud to Harry, but I smiled, amazed by the meaning of that sweet, ordinary gesture: buying a cake to share a moment and mark a milestone for himself and others. He had started something and followed through.

"Try Weinrich's Bakery," I suggested. I couldn't believe it had already been a year. As he walked out of the room, I was filled with hope and joy for him.

The next day, I followed up: How was the meeting? The cake? The celebration?

"Really good," Harry said. "We had more than fifty people."

As much as I wanted to share Harry's road to recovery, I knew I could not. I couldn't walk through his stepwork with him, couldn't attend meetings and hear his conversations with his mentors. But I could ask little questions and try to share in these small moments of accomplishment on the periphery of his journey. I wanted him to know I cared, that I was standing by, so glad to see him looking well and happy.

It was over the phone, a year earlier, that PJ and I had heard life coming back into Harry's voice. Now, a year later, I saw first-hand the brightness return to his handsome eyes—eyes that seemed to permanently reflect the glow of birthday candles on a cake. If I couldn't accompany him on his journey, his bright eyes and healthy-looking skin would be the report card for now.

HARRY

I could see now that not all had been lost. In meetings, I grew accustomed to talking to people of all walks of life, forming genuine friendships with men and women of all ages and races. Despite our differences, we all had something in common: a shared disease, the firsthand experience of humanity's imperfection. The experience had made me more open-minded. Watching your worldview—your entire belief system—shatter will do that to you. I learned that asking for help was more valuable than trying to "man up."

As my life improved, I saw how my family thrived without the constant worry I had caused in the past. My mom, growing in politics, diving into work that she loved so much. She could focus more fully on passing laws and helping her community. My dad, working hard and mentoring me in the bicycle industry. My brother Pat, promoted to a senior writer and deputy director of messaging for President Obama, working just feet away from the Oval Office. And Alex, making progress as an engineering major at the University of Miami.

I was making progress too. At work, I moved up from customer service to sales. Turns out, not being high or in the throes of withdrawal made the job much more bearable. I loved developing trust with our customers, fixing problems when a shipment went wrong or something was out of stock. I made deals, negotiated prices and payment terms, and showed empathy when there was a problem. I rebuilt my reputation, working hard until the rumors and truth of my past were overshadowed by the reality of the present.

With a little help from my parents, I bought a small row home in Ambler, a suburb of Philadelphia. I learned how to manage a budget, to make payments on time and in full, and to take pride in owning a space that was all mine. The house had three small bedrooms and a concrete façade with a small front yard. The living room was tight, filled with mismatched furniture donated by family and friends, but it was home.

Most of all, it was a space where my relationship with my daughter could blossom. She had her own bedroom, and you couldn't walk through the house without seeing one of her toys left on the floor. My daughter's mother and I were getting along. She was, and is, such a great mother. We were young and learning to co-parent, focusing on raising our beautiful girl while reestablishing our own lives.

On weekends, I would walk my daughter to the park at the end of the street so she could play on the playground. Or we would stay on the couch, snuggling under the covers to watch the same Disney movies over and over again. We never got bored. We talked about holidays, and family. We talked about animals. She loved snakes, just as I had loved them as a kid. I taught her everything I knew about them and took her to the local creek to search for them. Each day was an opportunity to grow closer, to learn about and to love each other more.

I was no longer satisfied with simply not using drugs. Checking off another day clean was something I never took for granted, but I came to see it more as a baseline, a foundation to build on. I had gotten a taste of the potential for my own life by watching friends do more than just recover. They were thriving, and I wanted to do the same.

MAD

A couple of years into my work as state representative, I had grown more confident in my voice. Caucus leadership appointed me to the Judiciary, Ethics, and Appropriations committees, where I focused on several issues that I saw as intimately interconnected: fighting for robust, equitable funding of education on one hand, and dealing with the fallout from when we fail on this central mission—pushing for criminal justice reform and funding to combat the dual epidemics of gun violence and opioids—on the other. As for the opioid crisis, I found myself more willing to speak publicly about it, especially when it came to helping fight the stigma that so often surrounds the crisis.

The numbers are staggering. Each year, gun violence steals forty thousand lives and wounds another hundred thousand people, with countless others terrorized and traumatized. Drug overdose claims nearly seventy thousand people annually, and that's before even considering many other forms of addiction.

Remember the world's response when two Boeing aircraft crashed within months of each other, one killing three hundred and forty-six souls? The world leaped into action. Under immense public pressure, government agencies forced the company to ground that plane. Overdose and gun violence should be no different. In each case, a jetliner of souls is crashing down on our country every day. How can we surrender to this, how can we accept it as our new normal? What we need is a similar response: an urgent grounding of the things in our society that fuel these crises.

In committee meetings, I spoke up about gun violence and criticized the use of mandatory minimum sentences—something our legislature and too many others were too fond of passing. As if we, from the comfort of our marble halls in Harrisburg, knew better than the judge and jury what action was appropriate for the person and offense in front of them.

There are other policies that can help stem the worst effects of the opioid epidemic. Government has a crucial role to play in passing them, paying for them, and implementing them. We should commit more dollars to the treatment of the disease— with full medical coverage including in the event of relapse. Imagine if a cancer patient suffered a recurrence of her disease and society said, "Nope, sorry, we've already treated you once.

You're on your own now." Too often, that's exactly what we do to those suffering through addiction.

And industry has a role to play too. The pharmaceutical companies who knowingly put sales and profits above right and wrong, life and death. They must be held to account, and beyond that, rise up and become a part of the solution.

Politicians and public servants have to get this right. But there is something bigger at play—something personal, not public—that our entire society has to get right. We have to see and embrace the humanity of those who have the disease of addiction. We have to confront our own fears. Too often, we would rather turn away and say "That's not my problem," because it's scary, it's fearsome, it's ugly and grotesque. But it *is* your problem. It is *our* problem. We are lying to ourselves when we say it isn't.

Every time I head to 30th Street Station in Philadelphia, there are the familiar, often young-looking people who are so clearly racked with addiction, begging for money, anything. We have a duty to look them in the eye, offer what we can, and let them know there's help available. It's all of our responsibility to make sure that happens.

My time in public service coupled with our experience at home with Harry lead me to one conclusion: It's simple. If we can see the human being inside the person with the disease, then we will make sure more and more people have the chance to recover. It is only when our public policies meet our shared humanity that we'll get this right.

HARRY

There was a girl in the marketing department who caught my attention. We were the same age and knew many of the same people, yet somehow we hadn't crossed paths until now. Her name was Juliet.

She was gorgeous, with long blond hair and dark hazel eyes. But her smile was what drew me in. A big authentic smile that creased her cheeks, forming a subtle squint that accented her eyes. When she smiled, you knew it was real. Not a gesture or forced courtesy.

Juliet was warm and caring, yet always wonderfully blunt. She never held back from telling you exactly what she thought. Especially when something bothered her. At the office, she would make fun of my haircut, of my sense of style. "You've got potential, but it needs some work," she'd say.

Juliet had never seen me high. She joined the company after I came back from rehab. I was grateful that she hadn't seen me at my lowest, though I have to imagine she heard some of my history from our mutual friends. As our conversations expanded and trust formed between us, I opened up, telling her the details of my past and the work I'd been doing to maintain my recovery. She received it openly, nonjudgmentally. It didn't scare her off.

As our friendship grew, I found reasons to pop back into the marketing office where she sat. I was always asking her questions that likely could have been handled by email. I just wanted to see her. I knew I had to be careful, though. In rehab and in meetings, they told you to avoid romantic relationships for the first year of recovery, and even though I was beyond that, I knew I needed to take it slow. As Father Bill always said, "Two sickies don't make a wellie." His point was that a healthy relationship must be built on a solid foundation, and that kind of foundation can't exist when one partner is too caught up in himself. Addiction drives you toward selfishness, and it can take years in recovery to break down those tendencies. I wasn't positive I was ready to care for someone else. After all, I had only just started to like myself.

As I thought back over the last year, I saw how fortunate I'd been before going into recovery. The truth is, I should have been in jail many times over. I've had police stop me and let me go without an arrest—stops that would have resulted in significant jail time for many others. That's something I've had to grapple with. It's not fair that I'm free and others are not.

What if I had been a minority, or from a different family? Would the police have been so inclined to send me on my way with a warning? The color of my skin, the address on my license, the car that I drove—they were the pillars that held together my freedom at my lowest moments. People always say life isn't fair. And they are right. I knew that intellectually, but it took recovery to show me which side of the ledger my life was on. Squarely in the unfairly fortunate column.

Around that time, my sponsor gave me something to do with that realization. He had been leading meetings in the Philadelphia prison system, hoping to bring the steps to inmates stuck behind bars. He suggested I do the same. "Yo, Har, ya gotta get in service if you want to stay clean."

I was hesitant at first. My sponsor had never steered me wrong—but what the hell could I offer these inmates? I never spent a night in jail, let alone prison. I hadn't even been arrested. Who was I to go speak with them? I was the kid whose privilege helped him escape the fate that had fallen upon them, the fate that I deserved. How would they receive me?

I thought about these questions until my sponsor told me that none of that mattered. The only thing that mattered was this: Was I willing to be of service?

So I agreed. Orientation would start in a few weeks.

MAD

In a random and fortuitous coincidence, I was on a bike ride with Michael Nutter, the mayor of Philadelphia, when he stopped to take a call.

Earlier that summer, it had been announced that Pope Francis would visit America. His itinerary remained unknown. Surely he would visit New York City and our nation's capital, but there was endless speculation over where else he might go.

The pope meant a lot to me. As a young woman, I had been drawn to John Paul II, whose papacy began one month before my father's sudden death. My father marveled that a pope could be younger than himself. Our image of the pontiff had always been an old man—Pope Paul VI—but John Paul II was handsome and charismatic, like my own father. And he spoke to young people like me.

In 1980, I had the chance to meet him at a mass and audience in Rome. As the pope passed my girlfriend Amy and me, I was able to touch his hand, look into his eyes, and say, "Good morning, Holy Father."

He paused for a moment while I shook one of his hands and Amy kissed his other. "Where are you from?" he asked.

I stammered, "Phil—phila . . . del-phi-a."

"The United States," Amy added.

And with that, he moved on.

Pope Benedict did not similarly inspire me, though I admired the courage it must have taken for him to retire. But when Cardinal Bergoglio, the unlikely candidate from Buenos Aires, was elected to the role and claimed the name Francis—signaling his humility, his mission to the poor and broken, and preaching God's love and mercy on us all—I was hooked again. His sweet face drew you in. It was the simple smile of someone overjoyed by joy, as I remember one author describing it. To this day, we keep a picture of Pope Francis on a corkboard in our kitchen, beaming among a crowd.

You know the look that overwhelms your face when you receive big news? I recognized a hint of that in the mayor's eyes as he wrapped up his call. After hanging up, he offered me a hug. And that's when I learned—unofficially and confidentially—that the pope was coming to Philadelphia.

This pope, visiting my home city! I couldn't believe it.

As a state representative, I attended some planning meetings and followed the pope's itinerary closely—a lineup of welcome events all across our area. Many of the places were ones you would expect: a seminary, the basilica downtown, a public mass on the Benjamin Franklin Parkway. But there was one stop on the itinerary that brought a smile to my face: a prison in Philadelphia. I had never heard of a pope visiting a prison, yet it seemed to me the essence of Christ's teaching. *For I was naked and you clothed me, hungry and you fed me, in prison and you visited me.*

No modern pope had done it, I learned. The last time was in 1958, when Pope John XXIII visited Rome's Regina Coeli prison during his first Christmas as pope. "Listen," he told his personal secretary, "my mother taught me that for the holidays we must not only go to mass, but we must also do works of mercy." Surely Pope Francis had taken note. By going to a prison, he was offering a powerful symbol of his faith and sending a message—not just to the inmates, but also to the people on the outside. He was lifting up their humanity and seeing himself in them.

As the plans took shape, I volunteered for anything that might ease or speed the pope's trip. Maybe I could help seat people at one or more of the masses, I suggested. Or maybe we could put someone up at our house.

But as the week of the visit approached, my hopes narrowed to one possibility. If the pope was coming to Philadelphia and visiting many places, my first choice—if I had one—would be to go to a prison with our pope.

HARRY

As I sat in the upstairs classroom of a Philadelphia prison, I looked around at the people gathered there. Twenty or so men and women of all races, giving up their Saturday to become authorized volunteers in the Philadelphia prison system. As a kid, I would get on Pat's nerves often, and he would respond by telling me I was destined for jail. Decades later, I had fulfilled that prophecy—though I'm sure this was not what he meant.

We sat at metal school desks as an instructor gave us the cold, factual do's and don'ts of jail. We learned about the precautions we needed to take to avoid accidentally bringing in anything that could become contraband inside—cash, cellphones, jewelry—anything that could be taken and traded among inmates. The instructor sternly reminded us that a handful of guards had recently been sentenced to prison for smuggling drugs to inmates.

When the class ended, we were sent downstairs for fingerprinting—a final stage of background checks before earning the necessary clearance. As I left the building that day, I was hesitant to wipe the ink from my fingertips. I saw it as a reminder of how unfair life can be—and how grateful I was to walk around as a free man.

A few weeks later, a volunteer spot opened up at Curran-Fromhold Correctional Facility. CFCF is the city's largest jail, housing around two thousand inmates at any given moment. It's well known throughout the area, and plenty of my friends and acquaintances had been sent there over the years. Still, I had no idea what to expect when I showed up to lead a 12-step meeting on that first night.

Driving in through the gates, I came upon an impressively large building, surrounded by the typical barbed wire fencing and concrete walls. There were floodlights in the parking lot and scarce few windows on the exterior of the building. I parked my car in the back of the lot and sat there for a moment, working up the courage to walk in.

I thought of my friend Mark, who was still in prison serving his sentence for manslaughter. I had visited him once before. He looked good—healthy, even—having gained back some of his weight. But I couldn't stop thinking of how our paths had suddenly diverged. In high school, we had done everything together, from bus rides to homework to drugs, and been pulled over by the cops more than once. If life were fair, we would be imprisoned together or clean together. That unspoken inequality was a reminder of how fragile life and freedom are. How thin the line can be between teenage fun and adult consequences.

Our interactions hadn't been easy. Mark and I talked as we always had, bringing up mutual friends and experiences and sharing who was doing well and who wasn't. We reminisced over high school and college, over the good times that all happened to be in the past. It made me realize how hard prison is. How hard it must feel to be stuck for years, watching life continue to move on without you. No matter how desperately I wanted to give my friend hope, I would never be able to save him.

At CFCF, I signed in and waited to be brought back to the meeting room. As I looked around anxiously, I watched the guards. Some looked serious, some were laughing as they carried on with one another. I kept quiet. I wasn't afraid to go through the locked doors, but I worried that the inmates might not get anything out of my visit. Why should they listen to me when they had been through far worse than I had? What if I got in the way of the message I was here to share?

At the main desk, I put my books and pamphlets into a tray before stepping through a metal detector. Another guard brought me through one locked door, then another, and another—a total of six locked doors. Then we entered a small classroom. There were posters on the wall, the kind you might see in an elementary school, showing the alphabet, grammar rules, and clichés about writing well. At the front of the room there were chalkboards with lessons half-erased.

I set up at a small desk in the front, carefully laying out the literature as a couple dozen inmates shuffled in. By the time the meeting began, I felt at peace. The locked doors, the barbed wire— all of that faded away as I reminded these men that I was no different from them. I was an addict. I told them my story of desperation and desire, of hopelessness turning to hope. But this wasn't about me or my story. It was about the promise of finding freedom from active addiction.

There was a long pause between the end of my talk and the moment when the first inmate raised his hand to share. But once one hand was raised, more quickly followed and the conversation flowed easily. Before long, this meeting was no different than the countless ones I had attended over the past year.

The hour flew by. I listened as the inmates told me their stories and asked questions about the program. Some talked about how they'd been arrested and why they were here. Others recounted their experiences with rehab. Most seemed skeptical—probably about me—and few of them were likely there just to get off of their block for an hour. A few, however, seemed genuinely interested. You could see the difference in their faces. They had a deep look of sincerity, while others masked their emotions through jokes and laughter, anger and frustration.

Soon a guard returned to take the inmates back to the block. I watched as these men were forced to walk back to their cells, many of them without a release date in sight. Plenty had been charged for simple possession, stuff I had done. The same life-altering charges could have been brought against me at almost any moment over the last few years, yet now I had a guard escorting me to freedom and a silly little badge that said I didn't belong in jail. Bullshit. My clean record bore zero relationship to the truth of what my character had been. As I made my way back outside through those same six locked doors, I remember feeling a strange mix of gratitude and injustice. I was separated from the inmates by six locked doors—and an endless list of unfair advantages.

I went to CFCF every other Monday night, bringing guest speakers whenever I could. I loved listening to the inmates as they shared their experiences and observations. One man said he had been clean and going to meetings for years, but divorce led to an unfortunate relapse, triggering a chain of events that landed him in jail. I could hear the sadness and desperation in his voice. He had known the joy of being clean, only to let it slip away.

The inmates often asked if I was paid to be there. Much to the guys' surprise, I told them I wasn't. "You're telling me you come to jail because you want to?" one guy said. "That's some sick shit!"

But I explained that I felt a responsibility to be here. That I had recently broken away from the vicious cycle of active addiction, and I would be selfish not to share my experience if it could help even one person. It sounded like a cliché, but it was true. I wanted them to see how the actions that brought them here didn't have to define them. We were all imperfect. We were all human.

Some of the men told me that they couldn't wait to leave. To see their kids and families, to eat real food again. They shared their dreams. They would do things differently this time, some would say. It reminded me of my time in rehab, talking to other addicts as we planned our return to society.

I could see myself in all of them. The meeting removed all of the barriers between us—age, race, drug of choice, and even the literal bars surrounding them. Often, the most meaningful part of our meetings wasn't what we said, but the sense of togetherness we felt. A sense that someone had come to see them.

MAD

Harry had told me about his volunteering at a nearby prison. From the moment he came out of treatment, Harry had used his own life experience to help others. Now here he was, doing so for a group of inmates. I pictured him going into that place, still looking younger than his years (despite a chest covered in tattoos), to work with men suffering from addiction. It was not lost on me—and I am sure not on Harry—that if it weren't for several things that I will not call grace, Harry could have been in their shoes.

I had visited local prisons before, including SCI Muncy, an

all-women's prison in Pennsylvania. There I met women lifers whose only wish was to die somewhere other than prison. Some were old women, convicted decades ago as accomplices, or under mandatory minimum sentencing rules.

I was proud of Harry, yet I worried for his big heart. Walking through those cold, clanking, dehumanizing gates armed only with compassion, experience, and empathy. He was a white kid from obvious privilege. That gave him a break, a break others don't get—and that's not fair. But maybe, like the pope's visit to come, Harry could become a messenger of hope.

In the days leading up to the pope's visit, I made an unorthodox request. Could I possibly attend the pope's visit with the inmates? I would do anything. Hold the door open, set up the chairs. Anything. The planners assured me they understood the sincerity of my request, but it was unlikely that they could make it happen. Very few people would get in. In the end, I was offered passes to the mass on Benjamin Franklin Parkway, and Pat was able to get me a pass to the White House grounds for the day when Pope Francis would visit President Obama.

On that crisp, beautiful day, I took the train to D.C. and stood toward the back of the White House grounds in the dense crowd. The pope walked out in all-white robes, set against the white stone of the White House balcony. I was thrilled to be there, even if the Holy Father was little more than a beautiful white speck from my vantage point.

Pat, I knew, was up there somewhere. Much closer to Pope Francis, if a bit further away spiritually. Later, he joked that he hoped to get close enough to fake a sneeze near Pope Francis, so he could receive—you get it, the ultimate papal blessing. After all those years of Uncle Wally saying mass for us in our living room, where did my boys go off the rails?

On the train ride home, I answered a call from a number I did not recognize. It was the lead organizer of the pope's Philadelphia visit. "Madeleine, you can go to the prison," she said.

I was shocked. I told her I did not know how to thank her.

We talked through the details. I would not be there to volunteer; they wanted me there in my capacity as an elected official, so I would not have the chance to hold the door for the pope. I could live with that compromise. "What prison is it again?" I asked. CFCF, Curran-Fromhold Correctional Facility, she said, on State Road in Philadelphia. How would I get in? "You've got nothing to worry about," she said. "We will do the security clearance. You will be on the list."

I thanked the organizer, hung up in tears, and turned my face to the window as the Northeast Corridor sped by in a blur.

After a few minutes, I called our family to tell them the news. "I get to go to prison with the pope!" I called PJ, Pat, even Alex. "Here she goes again" I imagined them thinking as their mother got carried away by some meet-and-greet with the pope. But I didn't care. My heart was bursting with joy, pure joy.

Finally, I called Harry.

"You are not going to believe it," I said. "I am going to be allowed to be with Pope Francis during his prison visit!"

"Really, which prison?" Harry asked with interest in his voice.

"Curran-Fromhold?" I said, trying to keep the name straight.

I hadn't considered that it could've been . . . What were the chances?

And yet it was! The prison hosting the pope's visit was the one where Harry had been volunteering. The prison both he and I knew could have been his own.

"Would you be interested in going?" I hesitantly asked, knowing there was little to no chance at getting a second spot for the prison visit. To be honest, I wasn't even sure if Harry cared. PJ and the boys had long distanced themselves from the Catholic Church, though I do think they saw that Pope Francis was different.

But Harry said yes. Again. I had no idea.

For the rest of that train ride, I debated what to do. The organizer had done me a great, great favor by getting me a pass to see the pope. How could I ask for more? But then I thought of Ed Rendell's teaching: If you don't ask, then the answer is surely no.

I called the organizer back. After breathlessly thanking her again, I asked if there was any way my son Harry could join me. "You see, I did not know it, but Curran-Fromhold is the very same prison where Harry volunteers every other week," I said, without elaborating on what he volunteered for.

With great patience, she said she was sorry, but she couldn't get another pass. So I asked if Harry, just Harry, could go in my place. No, she said again, I would have to be the one. She was working through a thousand details, a thousand requests. I was amazed by her graciousness in even considering my request.

I called Harry back. "I'm sorry, Harry, she said no." He knew the chances were slight, but I heard the disappointment in his voice. Now I felt guilty that I had the chance to go at all.

An hour later, still on the train, lost in my own swirling thoughts, I looked at my phone. The organizer was calling again.

"Madeleine, I was really touched by your son's story. I've found room for him. You can go together."

Now fully crying, I stammered a thank-you. "You have no idea how much this means to me. Thank you. Thank you."

And in that moment of joy and elation, those old, meaningful words from the mass came back to me: *Lord I am not worthy, but only say the word* . . .

On the day of the visit, Harry drove us to the prison in my car. We were running late. As we sped down Cottman Avenue toward CFCF, the road felt more like a runway. The roads had been closed, and Harry drove as though he wanted my six-speed BMW to take flight. He reasoned that my legislative license plate would get us out of a jam, but I did not want to test that.

As we neared the prison, we passed through a series of barricades and checkpoints before making it into the facility's huge parking lot. There was some confusion with the guards over why my last name was Dean and my son's was Cunnane, but they finally waved us through and told us where to park. It was a bright day, the sun reflecting off the imposing walls.

Inside, the guards took us to a holding area where coffee and juices were offered. We mingled awkwardly there for a while, moving between VIPs and the families of inmates. I was beaming, so proud to be there with Harry. I introduced him to the mayor, the district attorney, a future Pennsylvania Supreme Court justice, and some of my colleagues from the State House.

After a short wait, we were directed through a series of hallways to the large room that had been readied for the pope. In the center was a beautiful wooden chair that the inmates had handcrafted for the Holy Father, and rows of eighty or so seats were arranged around it in a horseshoe. On the pope's left-hand side were rows for the inmates' family members. On the right, rows for us. In the center, the inmates had been seated face-to-face with the pope. The joy in the room was palpable.

Harry and I sat together, with me positioned on the aisle, feeling incredulous. I didn't know about Harry, but as much as I'd wanted to be there—worked to be there—I couldn't believe this was happening.

HARRY

Like always, I felt out of place. I should've been seated in the center of the room, with the inmates—not between Philadelphia's district attorney and my mom, a state representative.

The walk into prison had been different this time. The guards were much friendlier to this group, a bunch of politicians and important visitors wearing suits, than they generally were to me when I arrived for biweekly meetings. They were smiling and welcoming, offering refreshments and a security search that was much less invasive than the ones to which I'd grown accustomed. This open room where we now sat was larger and brighter than any I had seen in the prison.

The setting was much more intimate than I had imagined. The news had been talking about the potential for a crowd of more than a million at the pope's mass on JFK Boulevard later that day. A striking difference from this room of maybe one hundred people.

The excitement in my mom's eyes was overwhelming. "Can you believe this?!" she kept exclaiming to anybody who would listen. As we mingled and took selfies with the other politicians, I couldn't wrap my head around the moment. Not any of it. Who was I to be here? Neither an important person nor an inmate. Just me. I thought of my uncle Wally, the masses he held in our house growing up, and my journey from faith to despair and back. Helped along the way by priests, rabbis, atheists—and now about to sit in the presence of the pope. In that moment, I realized that every step of my journey had brought me to a place where I could appreciate this experience with humility and understanding.

The crowd fell silent as the pope entered the room, flanked by his papal entourage. We presumed the inmates had been told to remain seated—to refrain from touching Pope Francis—and they kept to their space as he walked around the room shaking hands with them, blessing them. Then, toward the end, an inmate stood up, breaking the cycle and likely the rules, to embrace the pope in a hug. Then another, and one more.

When the pope reached our row, my mom asked him to bless the coin that I had received in a ceremony the night before I left Caron. It was a symbol of the completion of my treatment there. A coin that I had proudly given her as a token of accountability. I never imagined that this token that meant so much to me would one day be blessed by the pope as my mother watched, crying.

And I knew, in that moment, that miracles do happen. A miracle was keeping me clean. A miracle had brought my mom and me back together. A miracle of my own making—aided by the grace of my family, my friends, my treatment, and my faith that something better had been waiting for me on the other side.

MAD

The pope began his homily by thanking the inmates for receiving him, and by speaking about why he had come.

"Any society, any family, which cannot share or take seriously the pain of its children, and views that pain as something normal or to be expected," he said, "is a society 'condemned' to remain a hostage to itself, prey to the very things which cause that pain."

Then he taught from the Gospel story of Jesus washing the feet of his disciples. In those days, washing the feet of one's visitors was an important custom. The roads were unpaved, and when you walked anywhere, dust and dirt and little pebbles would stick in your sandals. Your journey would leave your feet bruised, cut, and dirty. Washing someone's feet, the pope said, was a sign of welcome. And to Jesus, it was a sign of an even more important truth—that none of us is above another.

The pope preached that life means getting our feet dirty. Sometimes we take the wrong path, like the inmates gathered in that room. But Jesus wants to wash each of us clean—to heal our wounds, no matter where our lives have taken us. "Jesus comes to save us from the lie that says no one can change, the lie of thinking that no one can change," he said. He offered those words to the prisoners, yet they were meant for us all.

As the pope finished his talk, he offered us a blessing. Then he greeted the prisoners, individually and quietly. We watched him move among the broken, offering healing and hope and a loving smile. Person after person, three or four rows deep. He then moved to the rows of family members, greeting each of them.

As he came down our aisle, I was holding in my hands Harry's Caron recovery coin, along with a mass card from Walter's funeral and a copy of the Beatitudes. When the pope came past us, I moved into the aisle—nearly blocking him with my body—determined to get a hug and proudly introduce him to Harry. The pope's warm face beamed and cast a glow on the two of us. And the words that came to me in that instant were the ones I had said so many times before: "Thank you, Holy Father, for coming under our roof . . ."

The pope's handler moved me aside, quickly yet gently. But in that moment, in that unlikely place, I knew that the rest of that prayer had already been answered:

Only say the word and our souls shall be healed.

THIRTEEN

BELIEVER

". . . the best is yet to be."

—ROBERT BROWNING

HARRY

As time went on, my self-loathing turned to self-love. I hadn't used drugs in three years, then four, and the promises that had been made to me in treatment were coming true before my eyes. My relationships were mended, and the desire to use had truly and fully been lifted. In meeting after meeting, I watched as other formerly hopeless addicts turned their lives around. These men and women had arrived with the blank stare of desperation, but their faces were now transformed—the life returning to their eyes. Hope.

Still, a recovery program doesn't, and didn't, save everyone.

The disease of addiction is chronic, progressive, and often fatal. While many of my friends in the program have relapsed and come back—showing up at a meeting looking distraught and willing once again to stay clean—there are some who will never have the opportunity to try.

Jon, crushingly for me, was one of those people. At funerals, people often describe their loved ones in the clichés we typically use to sum up a life. "He was the most caring guy I've ever known." "He lit up every room." But none of the platitudes does remote justice to Jon. He embodied every superlative you could think of: funny, smart, kind, the life of the party. But when I attempt to describe him or sum him up . . . none of it seems enough.

Jon and I got clean around the same time. I was new to the program, and he had just come back from a relapse. We clicked instantly. Some of the best times in my early recovery were spent driving to and from meetings with him, Jack, and Coles. When we joked and told stories about our misfortunes in active addiction, Jon had a way of finding humor in the darkest moments, always bringing us back to just how good we had it now that we were clean. Sometimes we laughed until it physically hurt, a potent reminder of the joy that is possible in recovery.

After a while, Jon relapsed, but we stayed in touch. He would come over to have a cigar on my porch, and we would stay up late talking about life. In these moments, he unleashed the humor that came so easily to him and opened up a bit more. We talked about parenting and relationships. We discussed our futures. He wanted to start a nonprofit to help addicts, or maybe get involved in local politics like my mom. No matter the struggle, Jon could put a positive spin on everything. He ended every phone call with "Love ya."

When he started using again, I would ask him what he was doing, but I didn't push him to get clean. I didn't want to make him feel that he needed to hide it from me. I wanted him to know that I understood, and that I was here for him, regardless. He had come back from relapses a few times already, so I understood that he knew what to do. I waited for the day when he would walk into the program, ready to start again.

But when our friend Dave called one day and asked if I had heard about Jon, my heart broke. I knew before he said anything else.

Jon was in a coma, Dave said. He had crashed his car while driving high and had sustained a traumatic brain injury. Doctors ran tests, trying to assess the damage, but it didn't look good. By the time I made it to Einstein Medical Center, Jon's family had learned that he wasn't going to recover. It was time to say goodbye.

Seeing Jon in the hospital was devastating. A young man, tall and strong, in his early thirties, now slipping away. His family surrounded him with love, knowing that all the love in the world wouldn't bring him back. I was reminded all over again of the unfairness of life. I'll never forget Jon, or the pain of losing him.

My first sponsor told me that the program isn't meant to be a revolving door for relapse. You are always welcome back, of course—but you never know when that door might slam shut forever. Fentanyl and the other drugs on the street are not as forgiving today as they once were. All it takes is one bad dose. That's how I've come to understand my recovery, the way I have to treat it every day. As a matter of life and death.

MAD

November 9, 2016, was a dark, rainy day. I was making coffee in the kitchen when Aubrey's mother called. Aubrey needed to talk to me. She was crying.

"Mama, did Donald Trump really win?" my granddaughter said through her tears.

"Yes, sweetie."

"But Mama, that's not right, that's not fair."

"No, sweetie, it isn't." Now I was crying.

"Hillary can win next year, right?"

I lied. "Something like that, sweetie."

Aubrey was five years old at that time, but with a grandmother and an uncle in politics, she had been to enough campaign events and White House visits to grow into a mini political junkie. She thought she was buddies with "Bawackobama," as she called him. All one word.

Aubrey had spent the summer and fall campaigning with me

for Hillary Clinton. She even got to meet the nominee herself at a small gathering of women and children in our district. Over tea at a local restaurant, Secretary Clinton engaged Aubrey, asking her what she cared about. "Twash on the playgwound!" Aubrey said. That was her issue. Clinton agreed. If my granddaughter had had a vote, the nominee would have won it right there.

I was crushed for Aubrey. She had been born while America's first black president was in office. How I wanted her second president to be a woman—a smart, strong woman.

I quickly called Pat. It was a rainy, drizzly day in Washington, too. Pat had gone back to work in the West Wing, and he said his co-workers were stunned. When I told him about Aubrey, we both cried.

A few minutes later, the president called the West Wing staffers into the Oval Office and gave them a pep talk. "History does not move in a straight line," he reminded them. "It zigs and zags." As Pat stood on the outer edge of the Oval Office carpet between the woven words of Kennedy ("No problem of human destiny is beyond human beings") and Roosevelt ("The welfare of each of us is dependent fundamentally upon the welfare of all of us"), he had a hard time getting through the meeting. He relays the story freely now. That he ugly-cried his eyes out as the president tried to console him and his colleagues.

It may sound cliché, but the presidential election of 2016 left me down and depressed—yet mad and motivated. I had wanted to run for Congress at some point in my life, but had let that chance pass me by in 2014, when I decided not to run for the open seat in my congressional district. I had only just pivoted from township commissioner to state representative, leaving my closest colleagues and friends mocking me for the seven months I'd spent on the job. ("Seven months . . . or was it seven weeks, Madeleine?") I was afraid to make another leap so soon.

Still, I felt an urgency to make a greater difference. Being perennially in the minority in the Pennsylvania House and Senate was extremely frustrating. We had no control over the calendar or what bills would come to the floor or have a hearing on. One example was our work on gun violence after the massacre at Sandy Hook Elementary School in Newtown, Connecticut. In session after session, my friend Representative Steve Santarsiero reintroduced a background check bill—HB1010—that he had tried passing before. But as members in the minority, we couldn't advance the bill. We urged the majority chairman of Judiciary to hold a hearing on gun violence. He agreed to hold the hearing as a compromise but said we could not mention the bill. We ended up hearing testimony from two Sandy Hook mothers, Francine Wheeler and Nicole Hockley. It was something—a chance to change hearts and minds. But I felt frustrated that we couldn't even talk about the legislation.

That morning in November 2016 gave me the push I needed to seek something more. After spending the next year examining my options, I announced that I was campaigning for lieutenant governor of Pennsylvania.

It was an odd race, a crowded field of seven mostly qualified candidates running in a primary against the incumbent Democratic lieutenant governor. News reports and an investigation by the governor's office revealed that he had let the office get away from him. He was caught up in the perks and state police escort more than the substance of his job. I campaigned on a different idea: If elected, I would not take the lieutenant governor's house. Instead, if I had my way, the state could turn the mansion into one of our "Centers of Excellence"—places of treatment that help combat opioid addiction.

I ran with the help of a small team at first, and always with my brother Bob at my side. We crisscrossed the state through crappy weather, in county after county. Inside me was enough foolishness to believe I could make a difference if our state's voters would give me a shot.

HARRY

The years I spent focusing on myself in recovery—living alone and taking care of my daughter part time—taught me how to find my own joy. It sounds simple, even silly, but it felt refreshing to sit alone in a room and feel content, without needing this or wanting that. To be happy with what was right there with me in the moment.

And yet, slowly, I sensed something opening up inside of me. My spirit was returning. I was shedding my chameleon characteristics, no longer disguising myself to fit in. I surrounded myself with men who taught me how to be a father, a friend, and a son. I knew there was more out there for me, like a growing family and a deeper kind of love. In recovery, they teach you to recognize that yearning and know when to reach for it.

When I felt ready to give relationships a try, I knew exactly what I wanted. A best friend. A woman of similar values and integrity. And I knew exactly who that person was.

Juliet and I had continued our friendship in the office, but so far I had held back. There were a lot of barriers that needed to be broken down. She had recently gotten out of another relationship. We worked together, and my father was her boss. I already had a child. And of course, I was in recovery, which meant we lived dramatically different lives. She went out with friends and drank. Meanwhile, I went to 12-step meetings.

Deep down, I knew none of that mattered. Juliet was worth it. When I spent time with her, I was the man I wanted to be. She gave me the opportunity to be myself: full of flaws, but striving to be better. After working through the pros and cons with my friends and my sponsor, I worked up the courage to ask her out.

"No," she said. She wasn't ready, wasn't sure it was right. "Not with that haircut," she added, trying to ease the discomfort of the rejection.

I wasn't deterred. Recovery taught me that all good things take time and effort. And I knew that a simple "no" wasn't the end. I tried going on dates with a few other women, in case my fixation on Juliet was misplaced—but each one was doomed. I couldn't stop comparing them to the potential I saw with Juliet. I hoped she might notice that I was letting my hair grow, changing the style she so vocally disliked.

In the meantime, I focused on our friendship, persisting in my interest but remaining respectful of Juliet's concerns. We talked about the challenges. What would it look like if it failed? Would we be able to continue working together? Could she drink in front of me if we went out? How would the relationship with my daughter go? I had been hesitant to bring any women around her in that way, not wanting to create any attachment unless it was the real deal.

The company often sent us on the road for sales meetings and trade shows. I was working in international sales, and Juliet was involved in event planning. Every once in a while, our travel over-lapped. At one point, we were sent to Taiwan with some of our co-workers for a new product launch and an annual trade show. I offered to drive Juliet to the airport, thinking it would give us an opportunity to talk alone before the fourteen-hour flight. On that drive, Juliet and I talked again about dating. I told her how I felt and what I wanted, but she was hesitant.

The flight from JFK to Taipei arrives early in the morning, often before the sun rises in Taiwan. And as soon as we arrived, it was time to get to work. Personally, I love the long flights. A rare op-portunity to disconnect, to unplug from the world and relax—even if I'm rarely able to sleep in the cramped economy section.

We arrived just before six, already exhausted but ready to work. The key to beating the jet lag is to keep moving that first day. Juliet and I had different agendas, so we split up. I took the two-hour drive south from Taipei to Taichung, arriving at the offices just in time for a day full of meetings. It was a busy couple of days, but it helped keep my mind from drifting toward the question of where things stood between Juliet and me.

Juliet left Taiwan before I did. As I was sitting in the backseat of a shuttle on the way to the hotel, she sent me a text.

"Okay, one date," she said.

And that was all I needed.

MAD

PJ and I were as harried as ever—him caught up in the work of growing a company, and me looking for a bigger political platform from which to make a difference. But we stopped often to marvel over Harry. He looked so happy, so healthy, thriving as never before. His wardrobe had changed for the better, and his investment in tattoos seemed to be slowing down. I noticed Harry saving money. Even his hair was coming back to normal. What a shift!

After a while, he started talking about a nice girl at work. Juliet had been a close friend of our neighbor Charlotte, who also worked for the bicycle company. Juliet was hired to replace Charlotte after she went to Penn for a master's degree. Harry said she was beautiful, but he talked more about her deeper qualities. The way he described her, she sounded fun, interesting, honest, and alive.

When the two of them began dating, Harry brought Juliet to the house—and, tellingly, one weekend, to Cape May. The boys, PJ, and I all admired the move. A weekend in Cape May with our family could be a test. We are a pretty lively bunch. All Saturday and Sunday, Pat and Alex and I looked at one another with darting, hopeful eyes. Could it be? Was Harry serious about this?

The weekend went well. Juliet fit naturally with our family of outgoing, sometimes outrageous personalities. And that first weekend turned into many weekends. I did worry briefly that Harry might get hurt. He had a daughter and a difficult history. Add a new relationship to the mix, and it was a lot to hold together.

Yet Juliet, eyes wide open, embraced all of Harry. When she saw how much he loved his daughter, she said, that was all she needed to see. Juliet noticed the strength and the good in Harry. She saw how much he cared. To me, that revealed not only her confidence in Harry, but more important, her confidence in herself.

One day in the kitchen—why does everything happen in the kitchen?—Harry asked me how much a nice engagement ring would cost. He wasn't ready to propose quite yet, but he wanted to know where he should go in case he wanted to buy one.

I tried to contain my excitement, but I could not. I gave him the name of a reputable local jeweler. A few days later, again standing in the kitchen as it all sank in, I stopped and consciously took the time to tell Harry what I thought: "Harry, with all the excitement around ring shopping, I wanted to tell you how happy I am for you. Juliet is not just a great pick. She is extraordinary. Daddy and I are so happy for you."

All I could think was how far Harry had come. How far we all had come.

HARRY

I knew early on that Juliet was the woman I wanted to marry. There was something about our relationship, a feeling that it was just right.

I watched as she developed a relationship with my daughter. They would play together, with Aubrey begging for airplane rides on Juliet's knees. When they read stories together, my daughter always interrupting with questions, Juliet would try her best to answer in a way Aubrey could comprehend. She fit perfectly into a complicated role, building a bond that was caring and supportive yet not at all overbearing. My daughter loved her. I loved her too.

After dating for three months, I survived the initial meeting of Juliet's family. This was far from a sure bet, considering my . . . résumé. I was a recovering addict covered in tattoos, with a daughter out of wedlock. But her family welcomed me openly and were instantly able to see beyond the surface. They accepted me as I was, and I loved them for it—even if they did make me take off my shirt and show all of my tattoos to the family, her grandmother included.

My mom and dad and I had talked about my intention to marry Juliet. When I was ready, the first call I made was to my mom. I had made a lot of calls to her during my young adult life, most of them conveying bad news. This time, as I dialed, I had a smile plastered across my face.

MAD

Harry went to the jeweler and described what he knew Juliet liked. A round solitaire stone. The jeweler told Harry he would bring in several diamonds for him to review the following week.

When Harry asked me to go along with him, I was overjoyed thinking of how far we had come: from doctor's visits and disciplinary boards to police stations and treatment centers, and now, shopping for an engagement ring. How far Harry had come.

As we sat in the jeweler's shop searching for the perfect diamond, another customer slipped into the shop behind us, silently browsing and overhearing our conversation. "I hope my son takes me along someday when he shops for an engagement ring," she said.

"Oh, I'm sure he will," I reassured her.

"Well, he's only three."

HARRY

By October, I was ready to take the leap. I'd had the ring for months. The only problem was that Juliet hated surprises, and she had a history of ruining her own birthday parties as a child. Not to mention that we were always together. I needed time and space to plan. The weekend before the proposal, I bought her plane tickets to California, giving her an opportunity to visit her sister and me a chance to run through the logistics. I called my brother Alex, and we found the perfect spot at a park in Chestnut Hill, a beautiful section of Philadelphia.

The morning of October 8, I woke up early out of excitement. Juliet and I had brunch reservations, so I drove over to my parents' house to pick up the ring and drop off my daughter. On the way, I told Aubrey about my plans to propose and said I would see her at the party later in the afternoon. She paused for a moment, processing this information. Then she asked, "Daddy, is there still going to be a party if she says no?"

"Of course," I replied. "It just might not be as fun."

At brunch, I felt so nervous and took too many trips to the bathroom to text Alex updates. He was waiting in the park, hiding behind the trees ready to capture the moment with his camera. I had downloaded four different weather apps in the days leading up to that day. They had all shown rain. I continued checking them throughout the meal, in hopes that we might get a small window of sun.

At the end of brunch, we paid the bill and walked to the car, which I had parked right by the entrance to the park.

"Let's go check this park out real quick," I said, trying to seem natural.

"But it's raining," she replied.

"Real fast," I promised. "Maybe we can take the dog here sometime."

She looked at me like I was crazy. But she went along.

As we walked around the pond, I started telling her how deeply I loved her, trying to sound as coherent as possible, repeating the speech I had been practicing in my head all morning.

As I dropped to one knee and showed Juliet the ring, I saw her eyes light up. And the smile that had drawn me from the beginning flashed across her face. "Yes, yes, yes!" she exclaimed. I slid the ring onto her finger and stood up to embrace her, overwhelmed with excitement and relief.

MAD

It was sweet to hear Juliet's delighted reaction to the grand surprise. The only thing that tipped her off were Harry's sneakers. Harry has a thing for sneakers. He collects them in the way he used to collect tattoos, and he keeps each pair pristine. Now here Harry was, in his newest bright white shoes, walking across a muddy park with Juliet. She sensed something was up long before he went down on one knee.

I was amazed at how quickly and confidently Juliet and Harry made their plans. Juliet knew she wanted to be married in Cape May. That's where their love grew, she explained, as well as her love for Aubrey.

As the wedding plans took shape, we turned our attention back to the campaign trail. It was one of the dreariest winters in my memory, but we kept going, crisscrossing the state. I spoke at area Democratic meetings, giving my stump speech over and over again. One night, leaving the third of four meetings of the day, I managed to hit a large pothole on a darkened Bucks County Road, blowing out both my front and rear right tires. Chris McCann, my lone campaign staffer, turned the scene into a makeshift campaign video as we waited for the tow truck to arrive.

The work was paying off. Each stop gave me more confidence that I could do this. Then, suddenly, the stakes got raised.

In late January 2018, the Pennsylvania Supreme Court declared that Pennsylvania's congressional maps were palpably unconstitutional. They advised the General Assembly to redraw fair ones. If we, the officials in Harrisburg, failed to draw fair district maps, the court would do it for us.

Montgomery County was likely to get a new seat, a seat of our own—which meant I might get a second shot at running for the United States Congress. Instead of being carved into five congressional districts, with not one of the sitting congressmen living in our county, Montgomery County would have a chance to send its own representative to Washington. After weeks of arguments in the courts and discussion in the Assembly, our county was granted that chance. Now I just had to decide whether to drop out of the lieutenant governor's race and go for it.

It was a lot to consider. By now, PJ's parents had moved to a nursing home near us in Glenside. It had been a difficult few years of transition for them. First, selling their big old house, moving them into a two-bedroom condominium in Jenkintown, until it became clear they could not live alone. She was frail and falling, and he was frail and forgetful, suffering from Alzheimer's disease. Yet they never forgot me or what I was doing: a state representative now running for lieutenant governor. When we visited them, Bill always said I was "built for" elected office.

One night, as I walked into this nursing home I'd visited so many times before, I saw a man I did not recognize seated in the lobby outside the administration office. He was beaming.

I said hello and introduced myself—daughter-in-law of Joan and Bill. He said his name was Wally. He was here applying for a job, hoping for a new start, a chance to do more. I liked him instantly. "Wally," I said, "I've got a good feeling about you. I hope you will join this place and the good they do."

And suddenly I had a good feeling about me, too.

With a newfound confidence imparted by that handshake with a stranger named Wally, I conferred with all of my usual top advisers, our election lawyer, my closest friends, and most of all, our family. A consensus was forming: A chance like this does not come around twice.

My best friend from the Pennsylvania House, Matt Bradford, offered to take PJ to lunch and offer his thoughts. Bradford counseled PJ that this race was going to be expensive, and we would need to invest as much money as we could in it in order to run strong. Bradford and I had watched our dear friend and colleague Steve Santarsiero run like hell in the difficult Bucks County race in 2016—a loss that dashed two years' worth of eighteen-hour workdays and placed untold stress on him and his family. Having worked so hard for Steve on a seat that was less winnable, however, Bradford believed that this was one we could win. PJ still calls it the most expensive lunch he would ever enjoy.

In the end, it was Pat who came up with the clearest assessment. "Mom, I never heard you wake up in the morning and say, 'I want to be lieutenant governor one day.' But I do know you have always dreamed of being in Congress. This is your chance."

He was right.

I loved D.C. and believed in the work that could be done in the halls of Congress. I remember going to Washington a few years earlier and visiting our congresswoman, Allyson Schwartz, on a session day. It was like something out of a movie. The congresswoman was busy with a vote, so her staff took me to an elegant room off the House floor. (I now know it as the Rayburn Room, where all kinds of formal and informal meetings take place.) I sat there, dreaming and yet never dreaming that I could make my way there. That place where I could have a national voice.

In the end, I changed course. I grabbed for the opportunity.

HARRY

Between my brother's job in the Obama administration and my mom's work in the State House of Representatives, politics was unavoidable at home. We are a family of strongly opinionated people who don't always see eye to eye. I consider myself more conservative than many of my family members, but I used to have little to no interest in politics. To me, politicians always seemed out of touch, distant from the communities they serve.

However, as I watched my mom work in the State House, I could see how dedicated she was to her constituents. She just wanted to help, whether it was staying late to talk with people after a community event or diligently researching a piece of legislation before casting her vote. When she introduced me to colleagues who seemed as dedicated as she was, my cynicism began to fall away. It was refreshing to watch—particularly amid the gross national political climate in the wake of the 2016 election.

When my mom got the opportunity to run for the newly drawn Fourth District, I was ecstatic. I wanted to help my mom reach her goal—Congress!—just as she had helped me reach mine. It was a challenging primary with lots of strong competition, but I knew that there was no better fit for the job than my mom.

As soon as she announced her campaign, we charged full speed ahead. With the new districts, there was less time to campaign than one would normally dedicate to a congressional race. In the ten months leading up to the primary, we would need to expand my mom's recognition well beyond the smaller district of Abington and Upper Dublin townships, where she had been serving as a state representative.

I scanned social media constantly, trying to get a feel for what the other candidates were doing. I paid attention to whether their tactics were working or not and looked for ways to improve our reach. Mom and I talked constantly about what we were seeing, where we could improve, and in what ways we might be behind.

We had something to talk about every day—and sometimes every couple of hours. Working together, toward a common goal. I was so eager to help my mom. To be someone who believed in her, just as she had been for me.

MAD

When the boys were young, I remember worrying that running for office would somehow steal their mother from them. I wanted to be a constant presence in their lives, and I knew we would not get to do childhood twice. My desire to be with PJ and the boys kept any notion of politics out of my head when I was in my thirties and forties.

Yet now, in my runs for state representative, briefly for lieutenant governor, and finally for Congress, I found just the opposite: The boys were contributing to me. They lifted me and my races. Nobody was taking from anybody. We were adding to one another.

The only complaint I heard from the boys was when they joked, "What's up with mom using her maiden name? Dean . . . Yeah, I get it. It's strong and fits on a yard sign, but what good is that going to do us Cunnanes when *we* want to run?"

Our family jumped into the primary with everything. The boys, and Stephanie and Juliet, were excited and engaged, everyone contributing in different ways.

Pat, the political operative, kept me motivated all throughout the race. *Mom, don't get distracted! Focus on this run. What are you doing today? How much money have you raised?* When times were tough, I trusted him to give me solid advice. First it was deciding whether to challenge one of my primary opponent's petition signatures. Later, I sought his counsel and ability to message when my Republican opponent took repeated sexist shots at me and lied about my husband. Pat is fierce in his loyalty and surgically sharp in his advice.

And Harry. My gun-owning son paid special attention to our social media campaign. Early and often, he would worry out loud about what we were and were not doing. He watched every post of my opponents and their followers, as well as the folks who decided to troll me online. I didn't look at that stuff. Pat couldn't look at it either, but Harry read every word. He was dogged in his engagement and support, promising that he would work the polls on primary day—with Juliet and Aubrey too.

And Alex. I could count on Alex for his cooler head—more than either Pat or Harry—and for his eye for what works. It was Alex who designed my first yard-sign logo years earlier, and through many races it remains largely unchanged. He is a creator with a marketer's eye for font and form, who is a few steps ahead of us all on style, communication, and cool.

In the end, we went into primary day with a three-way contest: Shira Goodman, the executive director of CeaseFirePA, with whom I had worked for the last six years on gun violence prevention in Harrisburg; Joe Hoeffel, the same Joe Hoeffel who introduced PJ and me back in 1978, when he was a leading Democrat in Abington; and me. Joe had served in Congress from 1999 to 2005, leaving to run first for the Senate, then for governor. After many years out of public life, he came back and campaigned on the strength that he would be ready for the position on day one. Over the last two months, we had appeared at dozens of debates, meetings, living rooms, nursing homes, and forums trying to make the case that each of us was best suited to represent Pennsylvania's new Fourth Congressional District. The winner of the Democratic primary would have a very good chance of taking the seat.

As my staff waited at home for the votes to be counted, I got a call first from Marcel Groen, the Pennsylvania State Democratic Party chair. Marcel, never one to get ahead of himself, reported fantastically good numbers for me at his polling places in Abington. Then, later that night, Joe called. He congratulated me on a good run and a win. He had conceded. More numbers came in. Shira called, too, conceding graciously like Joe.

In the end, I had won with 72.6 percent of the vote. That was the primary. A convincing win, but I still needed to get through the general election.

As we drove to the celebration that night, I reflected on the voters I tried to reach and the message I tried to send, the things I wanted to make a difference on in Washington. I returned to my list of "E's": educating our kids, growing the economy, protecting our environment, addressing the epidemics of gun violence and opioid addiction, and the ethics of those serving in office. The list had expanded in the time since I first ran for state representative, but these arguments were no longer abstract. They had become personal.

With primary day behind us, we ran hard, now with the wind at our back and a puzzling Republican opponent—a younger guy who seemed nice enough but had little connection to the community. He claimed to have made his fortune by shuttering businesses and then joining some buddy in short-selling stocks. My opponent spent a lot of time running against my husband. He claimed that our family was hiding millions of dollars "off-shore," and that PJ and I owned sweatshops in the countries that produced his company's bikes. That incensed our boys far more than it did the two of us. I remember Pat saying, "Mom, when you win, be sure and congratulate your opponent on the great race he ran against Dad. I'm not sure he'll get even one vote!"

It was funny, but it highlighted something I hadn't thought too deeply about in the moment. If I were a man running for Congress, would my opponent's main message have been against my spouse?

We ran all over the district, marching in parades, taking part in debates and public forums. With the help of so many people, we professionalized the campaign. It was a far cry from my first run for committeeperson at eighteen years old. I remember getting a text one night from Michael Nutter: "Mad, call me, I can help you. You need to use my TV guy, JJ, and my pollster in D.C."

A pollster? A TV guy? This was getting serious. There is a strange feeling that comes over you when you realize that you are going to need a commercial to get your face and your message out. It had to be good, Nutter said—a simple message, no cheese. He connected me to experts whom I trusted and respected, and still do. That's one of the puzzling things about running for office. People want to help. People in high places, people in less high places. People pitch in, in unbelievable ways.

All summer and fall, our house was overrun with campaign staff, and generous volunteers. People were poised on the sectional sofa, on the floor, in the bar. The dining room now a call center, our first floor was no longer our own. Some days, all I wanted was to have our house back to ourselves, but more often I was in awe of their help and commitment to the belief that we are better than our existing politics. That, as one of my heroes, Elijah Cummings, said just days before he died, "We are better than this; America is better than this."

As I looked around at the people making calls or assembling yard signs—volunteers whose names I sometimes didn't know— that was the thought I couldn't shake. We surely are better, I thought, and we will be better again. So long as Election Day went as we hoped.

As we barreled toward Election Day, I searched for places where I could find a few moments of downtime. One of those retreats was going to weekday masses, sometimes at the parish in my hometown of Glenside, Pennsylvania, other times in Harrisburg. I've always preferred the weekday ceremony to the one on Sundays. Just simpler.

On the Sunday before the election, I sat in my usual spot in the back, close to where I had always sat as a child. Having been so tied up in the campaign, I savored the chance to hear the Old

Testament, New Testament, and the Gospel readings. And I held out hope for the priest's homily. I needed the comfort of a good message this week, more than any other.

Lost in my thoughts, I struggled to focus and briefly tuned in and out. Until, suddenly, the priest moved on to an uncharacteristically political message. "Tuesday is Election Day, and you should not vote for anyone who is pro-choice," he said. "You must vote for candidates who have said they are pro-life."

I heard nothing more and walked out in a fog.

This priest had just told parishioners to vote for the party of Trump over me—the Church I had loved and defended over and over to my husband and sons. I was a child of that place. My father went to church and school here. So did Wally. I received all of my sacraments here, including marrying PJ and baptizing all three of our boys. I buried my parents and grandparents and everyone who mattered to me there.

They knew my heart, and knew what Trump stood for. As I walked out of church that day, I felt more like a stone statue than a child of that place.

Pat remembers meeting me at the house an hour later. I was sad. When I told him what had happened, he was furious, demanding that I stop going to a place that makes me sad. Through tears, I pushed back. "It's my faith," I said. "The Church is flawed, but not my faith."

Pat rolled his eyes, angry, and barked that I had better stop donating, at least.

HARRY

By the time Election Day arrived, everyone was more than ready. Anxious and excited, maybe a little nervous—but definitely ready. We woke up early to meet my mom at her local polling station. Cautious excitement filled the air on that cool, damp November morning.

We had planned for my daughter to join my mom in the polling booth and help her cast that first vote. It had become their Election Day custom. The difference was that this time, my mom was running for Congress—and, this time, I would be there to see it.

MAD

November 6, 2018. Finally, it was here.

We had a plan. Or really, Kathleen had the plan. Plans for how many polling places I would hit throughout the day, who would drive me, and who would be in the car. Staffers and volunteers would man each voting location throughout the huge district to greet voters and hand out our campaign materials. My brother Bob was with me every step of the way. The kids fanned out at different locations.

Unknown to me, the staffers from our D.C. firm, especially Jess, had a running bet with the in-district team. Who could keep me on schedule within five minutes, one way or another, through all twenty-six polling places? The winner got a good bottle of scotch, I'm told.

PJ drove us all over the area in his black Jeep Cherokee, with Jess, my smart, savvy, yet warm D.C. fund-raiser, directing our movements down to the minute. Three minutes at this polling place, six minutes here. "Mad, keep moving. Stop hugging," staffers would say. They all hated the amount of hugging I would do.

It was a happy yet hectic day, with different people joining us on the rides from site to site. The best was when Aubrey jumped in the car with me. Hand in hand, we strolled into a handful of polling places, saying hello to the people in line to vote. It was clear that Montgomery County was having an amazing day. Presidential-level turnout, in a nonpresidential year. Two years of pent-up anxiety had been deployed in this midterm election, giving our county the highest activity in the state.

As day turned to evening, I was visiting a polling place in Lower Merion with Aubrey when the damnedest thing happened: Rain began to fall, and a stunning rainbow shone above the building. A double rainbow, complete from one horizon to the other. I took it as a sign.

We climbed back into the car and headed to a few more stops. By the time we approached stop number twenty-two, the streets were dark and covered in wet leaves. Somehow we were still on schedule. I was betting on Jess. She had this.

Then, as we approached a stop sign in a dark, quiet neighborhood, our plans hit a snag. From the passenger's seat next to PJ, I saw it coming—a woman driving toward us from the cross street on our right. She turned the corner, aiming right at us, and never corrected her turn.

"She's going to hit us," I calmly said, as her car crashed into ours, scraping along the driver's side.

None of us was worried. The collision happened at less than ten miles an hour, and no one was hurt. PJ jumped out to check on the driver. "Are you okay?" he asked, with the rain coming down. The woman was older and apologetic, but she was fine.

PJ, sensing an opportunity, jumped in—right there in the middle of the rain-streaked road.

"Have you voted today?" he asked, trying to lighten the mood. She said she had.

"I hope you voted for my wife, who is right here, Madeleine Dean. She's running for Congress."

"Yes!" the woman said. "That's why I went to vote! I wanted to vote for Madeleine. I prayed that she would win."

We went home, out of time, skipping the last two polling places on our schedule. Later that night, we celebrated at Operating Engineers 542, Fort Washington, a labor union that had backed me—so warmly, like family—for all of my runs. The hall was packed with friends and supporters. It took a couple of hours for the numbers to trickle in, but when they did—

projected on a huge screen on the wall—it became clear that I had won the seat, with more than 63 percent of the vote. With that, the room exploded.

As I thanked the family, friends, and supporters that night, a thought ping-ponged around in my mind: *How did I get here?*

And I thought of what Abraham Lincoln said when someone asked him about his own success: "Someone believed in me, and I did not have the heart to let them down." That's how it was for me. That's the reason I won—the reason why anyone wins at anything. Someone believed in me.

HARRY

My wedding took place eleven days after my mom's election to Congress. Throughout the race, I had joked with her, "Remember, Mom, if you don't win, at least you have a great party eleven days later."

For thirteen months, Juliet and I had planned a perfect day in Cape May, New Jersey, the small shore town where my family had spent countless weekends together. We had picked our venue— a historic hotel called Congress Hall—before my mom announced her run for the U.S. Congress. Now it just felt like fate.

My wedding party had five groomsmen in it. Pat and Alex, my co-best-men, had been with me from the start. My sponsor and my friends, Jack and Coles, rounded out my groomsmen. As I slipped into my tuxedo that day, I couldn't help thinking that this day would never have come had I not agreed to get help on that Tuesday six years earlier. If I hadn't sought treatment, would I have survived to see my mom elected to Congress? Would I have been hiding my drug use at the wedding, like I had done at so many events? Would there have been a wedding at all?

The questions didn't matter. I was just grateful for the answers I had found: Juliet, my soon-to-be wife, whom I was crazy for; my brothers, family, and friends who supported me.

As we waited for the ceremony to begin, I thought of the friends I'd lost, but also the families that have been fortunate enough to receive a loved one back into their lives. No matter the circumstances, everyone deserves a chance to feel human again.

MAD

Our Lady Star of the Sea sits grandly in stone on the walking mall at the center of Cape May. Inside is a high-vaulted ceiling, creamy white and gold, and stained glass windows. I had always loved this classic Catholic church. On family vacations, I would go there alone when the boys and PJ refused to go. Now, on the day of the wedding, we would all be there together for once, again.

Ahead of the ceremony, we all met at the back of that beautiful old church. I loved the thought of the hour to come. Walking with Harry as he entered a future blessed by love, and family, and God. Harry, who had been through so much, who had persevered and found a new life.

As the handsome crowd of two hundred people took their places, PJ and I waited with Harry in the back. I had always been used to the traditional service, in which a groomsman walks the mother down the aisle while the groom waits at the front—second tier to the bride. But Harry had a different idea. "Mom, dad, I want you to walk me down the aisle," he said. He gave PJ and me a role to play. We had walked Harry into so many places—schools, jobs, rehabilitation—and he had walked us into a few, too. But none was as special as this moment, walking down the aisle with our son. Me, already in tears.

When we reached the end of the aisle, Harry took his place, waiting for Juliet at the altar. We took our seat in the first pew, and Aubrey climbed onto PJ's lap. And we watched as Father John Fisher, our friend and Oblate priest who knew Walter and us well, prepared to weave Harry and Juliet together in love and marriage.

HARRY

I remember watching my daughter walk down the aisle as the flower girl, in a beautiful black dress. She wore a nervous smile from ear to ear, so I gave her a small thumbs-up—a little extra encouragement to the girl who didn't yet know, and likely will never fully grasp, the mountain of encouragement she had been in helping me reach this point. The joy in her eyes provided me with hope and strength. We had grown so much in the past seven years together.

Then Juliet emerged from the back of the church, arm in arm with her mother and stepfather. She wore an elegant off-the-shoulder dress and carried a large bouquet of black and white flowers. A smile flashed across her face as we made eye contact. It felt as though we were looking at each other for the first time.

All I felt was gratitude. For her, for us, and for this moment of joy shared among friends and family. A moment suspended in time, when all sadness and worry disappeared. My nerves were gone. I was ready for "I do." As I looked into my bride's hazel eyes, I knew that nothing in my life had been wasted. Everything we had been through, together and apart, had brought us to this moment.

MAD

I struggled to compose my toast for the reception. I scribbled lots of things on scraps of paper, trying to collect my thoughts, but none of them felt right.

In preparation, I had read and reread my mother's long handwritten letter to me on the occasion of my wedding, nearly thirty-five years earlier. "This letter is to say thank you, Madeleine, for being a daughter who never disappointed, for one minute, your father or me," she said. "You are always a source of happiness and pride . . . you never had a temper tantrum and ate all your dinner. Or by the time we got to you, that was not an issue. Very big with Bobby, though—the experimental model. . . . We were so relaxed in our role as parents when we had you, that it surely contributed to your makeup. I know that Daddy is rejoicing, too, in what you have become."

As I look back now, I recognize that part of the reason I couldn't find the words was because I'd never taken the time to fully process what we had been through. I was still stuck in the mind of a mother, wishing that this had never happened. It took time to accept that Harry was right to see the good in the bad. The wisdom gained, against our will, through pain.

I thought of sentiments in my mother's note, and how different Harry's path had been. He was the second child, while I had been the seventh. He endured struggles that I could understand only at a distance. And yet, on his wedding day, we were rejoicing just the same.

I have no idea what I ended up saying. I left my notes on Harry's side of the wedding table when I got up to speak. The only thing I remember saying came toward the end—and I remember it because it was the same thing my mother wrote to me and PJ later in her letter. She ended by saying, as excited as we felt on our wedding day, "Truly, Madeleine, the best is yet to be."

That's how I ended my stammering wedding talk.

"As good as today is, Harry and Juliet—the best is yet to be."

HARRY

A couple months later, I walked with my mom through the tunnels that run underneath the United States Capitol. Busloads of supporters and constituents had traveled hundreds of miles to see her, and a line of visitors, buzzing with excitement, wrapped down the hallway to her new office—Cannon House Office Building 129.

I thought of how far we had traveled, too. Our whole family. My dad. Me, Aubrey, Juliet. Pat and his wife, Stephanie. Alex and his girlfriend, Alyssa. We were all there, taking in the scene. As cameras flashed and reporters barged in and out, my mom did her best to work her way through the line of guests and prepare herself for the official swearing-in.

MAD

In no time at all, I had gone from Harry's wedding to renting an apartment in D.C. and picking a suite in the Cannon House Office Building in a crazy lottery. Then the incoming representatives went to "Congress Camp," a series of sessions on everything from safety, to the rules of legislating, to the endless resources available to us, like the entire Library of Congress and Smithsonian Institution. They reminded us to ensure time with our families and make efforts to stay connected with friends. All week, we were bused around D.C. with police escorts. It felt surreal. Was that really my name on the heavy brass plaque on the wall outside the office: Cannon 129, Madeleine Dean, Pennsylvania? Impossible. Even after all the work of the campaign, I couldn't help feeling like an imposter.

As swearing-in day approached—January 3, 2019—our staffers rented two buses to be filled with friends, family, volunteers, young and old. We had gotten here together, and now we would celebrate together, too.

And yet a sense of greater uncertainty loomed above it all. The United States government was in the midst of the longest government shutdown in our history. An indefensible shutdown that was hurting millions of people. On day one, we would have work to do.

The day before the ceremony, my chief of staff, Koh, who

had worked with me since my state rep campaign in 2012, walked into my office. "Mad, head down the hall for a photo shoot," he said. "Take something meaningful with you."

Disoriented, I walked into the crowded room and was quickly matched with a photographer and a setting—heavy drapes and a dark desk. "What is this all about?" I asked the photographer. Turns out, it was she, Elizabeth, who had come up with the idea of photographing all of the women of the 116th Congress— House and Senate, Democrats and Republicans. The point was to show us in the traditional settings of power: stately, masculine, and now filled with the historic number of women elected to office.

I loved the idea. For the shoot, I wore my parents' gold eagle pin, the one my father gave my mother on their fifteenth wedding anniversary, 1960, amid the fun and promise of the Kennedy campaign. And I carried with me my Bible—Wally's Bible—the same Bible Aubrey would hold on the floor of the House tomorrow as I got sworn in. Tucked inside that Bible were Wally's life and death card, the Beatitudes, and of course, Harry's coin from Caron.

HARRY

For the swearing-in, my mom was permitted to bring one child onto the floor and another guest to sit in the gallery. I was thrilled that Aubrey would be with her on the floor to experience this piece of history. And I was honored when my mom asked me to be the one who sat in the gallery.

The members of the newly elected 116th Congress stood on the floor of the House and swore their oath to the Constitution in unison. I watched my mother repeat those words with my daughter standing proudly at her side. After all we had been through—the struggles and the overwhelming triumphs—I had never been so proud to be her son. I thought back to my wedding reception, when my mom gave her speech as the mother of the groom, and I raised my glass of nonalcoholic sparkling cider, toasting an amazing life. A life that's never easy, but always rewarding. A life that I never would have imagined for myself when my parents drove me to Caron on the day after Hurricane Sandy. Maybe that's what my mom meant when she wrote in that card on the quiet car ride, six years earlier: "Nothing is impossible."

Even today, I believe there is something more to come—something greater—for both of us.

ACKNOWLEDGMENTS

We never imagined that our experience might one day be the stuff of a book. So thank you, David Larabell, for driving from New York to our Philadelphia suburbs that summer day and sitting with us on the patio. Thank you for seeing a book in our struggles, seeing the hope in our story, and seeing the chance—just maybe—to help someone else.

Thank you to David's colleagues at CAA—Jamie Stockton, Jonas Brooks, and the rest of the team—for your professionalism, always seasoned with warmth and good humor.

Derek Reed! Thank you for your understanding of the message that we hoped to share from the very beginning—even before we could fully see it ourselves. For putting up with this mother-son team; for your ability to gently encourage us to search deeper, to work harder, and to always see the light in the darkest chapters. Your work has undoubtedly made this memoir more meaningful—not just for the reader, but for us. Thank you to your entire team at Convergent: Tina Constable, Campbell Wharton, Ashley Hong, Steven Boriack, Jessalyn Foggy, Vincent La Scala, Amelia Zalcman, Jessica Bright, Jo Anne Metsch, Emily DeHuff, and all the folks at Penguin Random House for believing in us. You have been our beacon, filled with the faith that our story might help others. You saw blessings in our pain.

We think especially of the families we have met along the way who have exposed their own pain, stumbles, ignorance, loss, and joys. The families searching for answers, and needing hope. Families experiencing the joys that recovery brings. And the families who have lost loved ones to the disease of addiction.

From Madeleine: I think of our loving friends, many of them lifelong, and family members, too. You had no time for judgments, your only wish was for love and health. Thank you.

I think of and thank the people I have had the chance to work with in teaching, politics, and public service—many who have become friends and family. Thank you for your friendship and heart.

And about our own family: None of this would have been possible without PJ—whose endless optimism, drive, and love made this story possible. I'm lucky to have gone from extraordinary parents, Mary and Bob Dean, to an extraordinary partner and husband, PJ. It doesn't get much better.

Except it did. We had Pat, Harry, and Alex. They are a better us, now joined by Stephanie and Juliet, and best of all, our grandchildren Aubrey, Ella, and Sawyer. Aubrey, know that you are the inspiration here. And Harry, lucky me to have gone this way with you. What a gift to work through our words and story together. And Alex and Pat. As different as all you boys are, you share one thing: a constancy of love. A love of family, of Harry, of us. You were and are our glue. No better parents' blessing. I love you and am proud of you.

From Harry: I'm forever grateful to my amazing wife, Juliet. Thank you for seeing more in me than my broken past, and for the beautiful life that we are building together. For finally saying, *Yes.* I love you more than I could ever write. My daughter, Aubrey, who may never fully grasp the impact that she has had on my life. My son, Sawyer, who was born while I was writing this book, may he never have to see that version of me. The three of you inspire and empower me always.

Thank you to my mom and dad, for always being there for me, and for growing with me through this process. Our bond is forever deeper through the writing of this book. Thank you for believing in me.

To the friends I've lost, and those that they left behind. To Jon, and Liam. To Caron Treatment Centers, and Little Creek Lodge, where my life began to change, and to recovery for giving me hope and love when I didn't believe I deserved it. Without the strength of my family, friends, and sponsor, none of this would have been possible.

Finally, we are thankful for what the process of writing and rewriting this book has meant to us. It has forced us to put our experience into words and has taught us more about ourselves, our stumbles, and what we have learned through the pain. As reluctant as I, Mad, was to live this experience—how I wished this pain could have passed us by—I now see how much we gained. Harry taught me that, when he wrote he would not change a thing. It has been in reliving it—that as Aeschylus said, I had to learn there is wisdom won though pain. Reluctant as we were, here we are, and we are the better for it.

And our closing thanks is to Pat. We know you opened to this page first—and with good reason. There would be no *Under Our Roof* if not for you.

You wrote your first book, *West Wingin' It,* after six years of work in the Obama Administration. Not just because you worked there, but because of your talent for writing and your surprising insights and heart. When your agent and friend David Larabell asked a couple years later if you were ready to write your second book, you said: "No, but my brother and mother might have an interesting story to tell." That's what sent David on his way to our patio that summer day. You believed our story might help restore or save a life. Just as it did ours.

You believed in us and convinced others along the way. So, oh yes, thanks, Pat.

With Love,
   Mad and Harry

ABOUT THE AUTHORS

MADELEINE DEAN is the congresswoman for the Fourth District of Pennsylvania, suburban Philadelphia, a member of the House Judiciary and House Financial Services Committees, and vice chair of the Bipartisan Women's Caucus. From 2012 to 2018, she served in the Pennsylvania House. From 2001 to 2011, she taught writing at La Salle University, and her writing has appeared in *The Philadelphia Inquirer,* the *Philadelphia Daily News,* and other regional publications. She and her husband, PJ Cunnane, live in Jenkintown, Pennsylvania, and have three sons, two daughters-in-law, and three grandchildren.

mad4pa.com

Twitter: @madeleinedean

HARRY CUNNANE has been an active member of the addiction recovery community since his recovery began more than eight years ago. He participates in a twelve-step program and volunteers at rehabs and jails around Philadelphia to spread a message of hope. Cunnane now works as a resource director for the same treatment center where he originally sought help for his own addiction. He lives in Audubon, New Jersey, with his wife, Juliet, his daughter, Aubrey, and their son, Sawyer.

Twitter and Instagram: @harrycunnane

hopeempowerschange.com

ABOUT THE TYPE

This book was set in Caledonia, a typeface designed in 1939 by W. A. Dwiggins (1880–1956) for the Merganthaler Linotype Company. Its name is the ancient Roman term for Scotland, because the face was intended to have a Scottish-Roman flavor. Caledonia is considered to be a well-proportioned, businesslike face with little contrast between its thick and thin lines.